A DEVOTIONAL JOURNEY THROUGH JESUS' FAREWELL ADDRESS

# FRESH FROM THE TABLE

NAN CORBITT ALLEN

A DEVOTIONAL JOURNEY THROUGH JESUS' FAREWELL ADDRESS

# FRESH FROM THE TABLE

NAN CORBITT ALLEN

FRESH FROM THE TABLE: A Devotional Journey through Jesus' Farewell Address



ISBN: 978-1-61715-632-8 print

978-1-61715-633-5 eBook (ePub, Kindle)

First Printing 2026

Editing and typesetting by Rick Steele Editorial Services, Ringgold, GA (https://steeleeditorialservices.myportfolio.com)

Cover Design by Amber Weigand-Buckley

Printed in the United States of America

## Dedication

To my husband, Dennis, who is now sitting at heaven's table with the Lord. He has always cheered me on, and I know he's continuing to do that from his heavenly mansion. Save me a place, honey!

To my sons and their families for showing me what it is like to cherish lives so precious that it's hard to fathom.

To the church families to which I've been privileged to belong and who planted God's Word in my heart since the day I was born.

## Acknowledgments

Thank you, Amanda Jenkins at AMG for believing in this project and to Rick Steele for the great editing work.

## About the Author

NAN CORBITT ALLEN has written over one hundred published dramatic musicals, sketchbooks, and collections for various music publishers and is a three-time Dove Award winner for musicals written with her late husband of fifty years, Dennis.

Nan holds a Masters Degree in English and Creative Writing and has taught at Truett McConnell University for the past ten years. Nan lives near South Nashville, Tennessee.

Contents

## INTRODUCTION

Family dinners. There's something about them that brings feelings of warmth and bonding. Most of our table gatherings consisted of immediate family, but sometimes it included extended family and friends. Table talk and delicious food connected us and made for relationships that instill precious memories to this day.

Jesus gathered with His "family" of disciples to celebrate His last Passover in Jerusalem, and the purpose of this meal involved the farewell address that followed. It was a time of connection, of questions and answers, of instruction, and of making memories that would serve to shape a new path to God's kingdom.

All four gospels frame the scene, but only the apostle John recorded the words of Christ as He tried to leave His followers with fresh words, and often reiterated things that He had already taught them.

By looking closely at this famous after-dinner speech, we can perhaps reconnect with the Father who stands at the head of the table inviting us to join.

You may want to use this resource around your own dinner table, sharing it with friends and family. If you have children at the table, I have provided some age-appropriate discussion questions for you to use. Also, if you want to go deeper into the Word, I have provided more scriptures tagged as "More Food for Thought."

Bon Appetit!

## DAY ONE

*Taste and see that the Lord is good. (Psalm 34:8)*

Little did the disciples know this would be their last Passover with Jesus. He had sent them to a specific man whom He knew would allow Him and His disciples to celebrate the meal at this man's house (Matthew 26:18). How surprised they must have been when Jesus Himself started to perform the traditional act of foot washing! Sure, this was a customary act before a meal in Jewish households, but never would the host of the meal carry this out for the guests. Servants were customarily employed to do such a dirty job. Nonetheless, after traveling around with Jesus for three years and witnessing many awesome and miraculous works at His hands, they may have been used to His departures from the norm even when they had no clue why He was doing what He was doing. So, the disciples lined up, waiting their turns. But when it came time for Peter to have his feet washed, as Peter was known to do, he opened his mouth with a bewildering question.

"Lord, *You* are washing my feet?" (John 13:6 emphasis added).

Jesus probably didn't even look up from what He was doing. "What I am doing, you do not realize right now, but you will understand later" (John 13:7).

The disciples didn't quite get it sometimes. For instance, in some of the parables, the men couldn't decipher the meaning themselves. In Mark 4, in the Parable of the Sower, the disciples asked the meaning after they heard it, but only after the crowds had left. Perhaps they didn't want the embarrassment of saying out loud that they didn't understand.

It's no shame to have questions. As 21st century believers, we will have to be content to let some questions go unanswered. We may, however, affirm the fact that, for now, what we can know will have to be enough.

There is so much that we cannot comprehend right now, and unfortunately, it's our nature to try to figure things out and control them. That doesn't mean we should stop asking or seeking. In fact, it means that we should keep searching and discovering, realizing that we'll only discern in faith what He wants us to know.

Do you have to know everything to believe in or trust God? If so, there is no need for faith. Paul addresses this when he writes about our hope of salvation that we receive by faith. Read Romans 8:24, 2 Corinthians 5:7, and Hebrews 11:1. What are these verses saying about having faith?

Allow yourself the freedom to trust Him without having to know everything about Him.

### PRAYER

*Father, thank you for inviting me to the table. Nourish my soul daily from Your word. Direct my way when I don't see the path clearly. Remind me of Your presence when I don't understand Your methods.*

### DISCUSSION

1. Do we have to know everything about Jesus to believe Him and trust Him? Why or why not?

2. What questions do you have about Jesus?

3. What is the best place to learn more about Him?

## MORE FOOD FOR THOUGHT

1. Read Exodus 12. What is the tradition of the Passover Meal? What does it commemorate?

2. Read Matthew 26:20–35; Mark 14:12–31; Luke 22:7–23. All three of these Gospel accounts record the Last Supper. How do they differ?

## DAY TWO

*Do not let your heart be troubled. . . . (John 14:1a)*

These are the first words of this lesson. Most English translations use the word "troubled" here in this verse, but *The Message* paraphrase puts it this way: "Don't let this rattle you." In other words, don't be alarmed or surprised by what I'm about to do.

Christ shared these words during a special holiday, the Passover. Though it had its somber elements, it was still a certified celebration. So why would the disciples' hearts be troubled? Why would Jesus address their fears and dismay? Why would they be "rattled?" Well, He had just reminded them—again—that He would be leaving soon. He said, "Where I am going, you cannot come." (John 13:33) This was a surprise and a bit disconcerting to those men who had dedicated their lives to Him and His ministry. Abandonment was not part of their plan. *Stay here and set up a kingdom*, they imagined. After all, Jesus was only 33 years old—in the prime of life. Apparently, He knew what kind of agony He would endure and how utterly defeated they would be without Him. So, He felt like He should prepare them—again—and console them.

That's the way a relationship with God works. He is the one to bear our burdens and soothe our hearts. The psalmist writes (Psalm 34), "The Lord is near to the brokenhearted/And saves those who are crushed in spirit." In a touching testimony from a psalm writer, "You have taken account of my miseries; Put my tears in Your bottle." It might seem to be an over-personification of the Almighty, but I love this statement. He not only *sees* our tears, but He "captures" them. No heartache goes unnoticed, and every tear that falls from our eyes, He will catch.

When bad news strikes, it's natural to be troubled (or rattled). The psalmist writes in Psalm 112, "They [people who love the Lord] do not fear bad news; they confidently trust the LORD to care for them."

The eighth chapter of Romans is filled with promises that speak to the issue of being "rattled" by circumstances. Here's just a few:

> And we know that God causes all things to work together for good to those who love God, to those who are called according to *His* purpose." (v. 28)
>
> If God *is* for us, who *is* against us? (v. 31)
>
> Who will separate us from the love of Christ? *Will* tribulation, or trouble, or persecution, or famine, or nakedness, or danger, or sword? (v. 35)
>
> But in all these things we overwhelmingly conquer through Him who loved us. (v. 37)

## PRAYER

*Lord, during difficult times, soothe my soul, catch my tears, and hold me close to Your side.*

## DISCUSSION

1. What does it mean to trust God and depend upon Him?

2. How can I talk to God or Jesus?

3. Can He help us when we are afraid?

## MORE FOOD FOR THOUGHT

1. In Isaiah 41:10, the prophet writes on this subject. Read it and note what it says about fear.

2. In Psalm 56:3, what does the psalmist suggest we do when we're afraid?

3. In Psalm 27:1, why should we not be afraid?

4. In Psalm 56:8, to what extent does God go to bear our burdens?

5. Read Psalm 23. Have you ever tried to memorize this lovely shepherd's song? Many use this to allay fears or grief. Try to remember it during difficult times.

## DAY THREE

*Believe in God...believe also in Me. (John 14:1b.)*

Believe. This kind of belief mentioned here has never meant to affirm the existence of someone or something. It implies much more than that. It must include total surrender.

In the late 18th century, Christian missionary and Bible translator, William Carey, felt called to leave his home in England to minister to people in India. In Carey's lifetime, both he and the mission he began printed and distributed the Bible in whole or portions in over thirty languages and dialects.

One of the stories told of him is that during his days of translating, he struggled with the way to convey belief in one of the languages. A faithful but exhausted native assistant of Carey's came into the tiny office and threw his whole weight onto a nearby cot. Carey had an idea. He asked the man, "How would you describe, in your language, what you just did, casting your whole self on that bed?"

Casting all we are upon Him is a close definition of belief that Jesus was talking about. Since surrender is not taught to us and, perhaps, isn't in our DNA, the idea of giving ourselves fully to something or Somebody is a barrier in these days. I believe that is why so few actually believe the way Jesus said we should.

"... believe also in Me." A short end to the opening of His first words at the table, but it has a deep meaning. If Jesus *was* God incarnate, as we believe, why would He delineate between Himself and the Father? The idea of the Holy Trinity is something we barely understand now, but at the table, those disciples were perplexed to hear that Jesus and their Father were one and the same. Yes, they believed in Yahweh. They had grown up knowing, believing, and studying about God. They had witnessed miracles and heard the teachings of Jesus, but seeing Him as the Father was still a mystery.

Several times Jesus would say that He was God in flesh; however, this was considered blasphemy in Jewish circles. How could Yahweh Himself be walking among us?

The prophet Isaiah said that the Messiah would be called "Emmanuel" which means "God with us." When this prophecy was repeated to Joseph (who was engaged to Mary) in a dream, the angel told Joseph to name Him Jesus. But the angel also said that "they" will call Him Emmanuel? Could He be called both? And why two names?

His proper name meant one thing (God saves), and His prophetic name was Emmanuel (God with us.) These two names together are the essence of the gospel. God came to earth as a Man with His mission to save many from eternal death.

He is still with us today. Not in bodily form, obviously, but in Spirit. He is still saving people. He is as close as ever.

James 4:8 says, "Come close to God and He will come close to you."

### PRAYER

*Oh Jesus, Emmanuel, I long to know more about You as I seek my Creator's face. Because You and the Father are One, I place my whole self upon You. I believe totally on Your ability to save me and sustain me.*

### DISCUSSION

1. Are God and Jesus the same?

2. How is that?

3. When talking to God are you also talking to Jesus? Why or why not?

## MORE FOOD FOR THOUGHT

4. Read James 2:18–20; John 20:29; Matthew 21:22; Hebrews 11:6. Why is acknowledging the existence of God not belief?

## DAY FOUR

*In My Father's house are many rooms; if that were not so, I would have told you... (John 14:2)*

One translation says that Jesus used the word "mansions" here, although closer scrutiny of the original language translates "rooms." I personally liked mansions better for obvious reasons, but when I unpack these words, I am even more impressed with this notion.

In this part of the speech, Jesus isn't referring to an actual dwelling—with a roof, a front door, a bedroom. He's talking about taking His beloved to be with Him forever. In His eternal care. In heaven.

Traditionally, the father at a Jewish wedding would offer his son or daughter a room he had built on to his own house. The newlyweds could live under their father's house—protection, provision, and proximity. This is what Jesus was referring to—an annex or addition onto His own dwelling—heaven.

One Bible commentator puts it this way: "He reminded His men that He would prepare a place *for* them and that He was preparing *them* for this place."

How long would this **preparation** of heaven take? Preparation for any event, like a wedding, could take months. Any special occasion, like a Thanksgiving dinner, could take days. Jesus' words here implies that the prep had not happened, but that it was imminent. Was there no heaven—yet? Obviously, this is not what Jesus meant. Genesis 1:1 says, "In the beginning God created the heavens and the earth." So, heaven was already there, but Jesus' statement means that He is taking care of all the arrangements for when we get ready to go there. Though we only have a tiny glimpse of what heaven will be, we can be confident that we have our reservations guaranteed and that the accommodations will be more than adequate.

You'll never find your room on your own. Let Him be responsible for escorting you to your final destination.

**"...If *that* were not *so*, I would have told you."** 2b.

The last half of this verse I believe is the most amazing promise of all. Considering His audience, the eleven men left at the table, He wanted to remind them that He had never lied to them before, and He would never tell them anything but the truth. In fact, He describes Himself as "...a man who has told you the truth, which I heard from God" (John 8:40). He is not only claiming His own trustworthiness, but God's inability to lie. How can you know that? Jesus said, "If you continue in My word, *then* you are truly My disciples; and you will know the truth, and the truth will set you free" (John 8:31–32).

What promises of His do you claim? His constant love? His sustaining hand? His overwhelming power? All of this is available to those who believe.

### PRAYER

*Lord God, thank You for providing me an eternal home when I am gone from this earth. This promise gives me hope and peace knowing that You have a place reserved for me in heaven.*

### DISCUSSION

1. What do you think heaven is like?

2. How can you know that you are going there?

## MORE FOOD FOR THOUGHT

1. Read Psalm 103:19; Revelation 21:4; Revelation 4:8–11; Revelation 7:9–10; 1 Corinthians 2:9 to be inspired about your heavenly home.

## DAY 5

*"I am coming again and will take you to Myself, so that where I am,* there *you also will be." (John 14:3)*

Whatever you believe about the Second Coming of Christ—the order in which it will happen, who gets to go to heaven first, who will suffer the tribulation to come on earth—that is not addressed here. It does address one thing: He is not only our Host, but He will be our Guide into our new residence.

It's all right to fear the unknown, especially heaven or hell, because these events can only happen after we die or after Jesus comes again to take us back with Him. But when we realize that He will be with us every step of the way, we can rest in the promise that we will be with Him forever.

When Jesus comes again, or if you die before that, He'll be with you through it all. This beautiful passage from Psalm 139 (*The Message)* is a prayer.

God, investigate my life;
get all the facts firsthand.
I'm an open book to you;
even from a distance, you know what I'm thinking.
You know when I leave and when I get back;
I'm never out of your sight.
You know everything I'm going to say
before I start the first sentence.
I look behind me and you're there,
then up ahead and you're there, too—
your reassuring presence, coming and going.
This is too much, too wonderful—
I can't take it all in!

Even death cannot separate us from God. In fact, when we go to heaven, we'll be with Him forever.

> Be strong and courageous! Do not be terrified nor dismayed, for the Lord your God is with you wherever you go.

That passage is from the Book of Joshua (1:9), but it is repeated elsewhere in the Bible.

What a reassuring thought—that God is always with us!

### PRAYER

*Eternal Father, I am overwhelmed when I think that You, God of the Universe could care about me. And that You are constantly with me wherever I go.*

### DISCUSSION

1. What are you most afraid of?

2. Can you imagine God being with you always, even though you cannot see him?

### MORE FOOD FOR THOUGHT

1. Read these scriptures about the Second Coming of Christ: Matthew 24:30–36; Revelation 19:11–16; 1 Thessalonians 4:16–17: 1 Thessalonians 5:2.

## DAY 6

*'And you know the way where I am going.' Thomas said to Him, 'Lord, we do not know where You are going; how do we know the way?' Jesus said to him, 'I am the way, and the truth, and the life; no one comes to the Father except through Me.' (John 14:4-6)*

Leave it to Doubting Thomas to ask a question that no one else was brave enough to ask. However, I'm glad he asked this for Jesus' answer has become one of the foundations of our faith. It could be that Jesus was frustrated, or He was making light of Thomas' questions. "How do we know the way?" "I *am* the Way," He spoke (emphasis added). Not, *I'll point the way,* but *go with you all the way*. He goes on to say, that He is the truth and the life.

Voices of the "world" (secular, not spiritual) keep calling out to us to get us to buy into its values and lifestyles. And even these aren't consistent. They change sometimes daily based on what someone has "discovered." We tend to chase the shiny new idea that comes along—it may sound good and promises to make our lives complete. But so many times these things, passed off as truth, are lies or half-truths that are warped philosophies.

Next, Jesus says that He is the life. Have you ever visited or even imagined a place that is perfect? And for a moment you sighed and said, "This is the life!" Who knows exactly what Jesus meant by this? However, it is a refreshing thought to know that all life (earthly and heavenly) can be found by trusting Him. It's the only way to really know the Father in heaven.

Finally, Jesus says, "...no one comes to the Father except through Me." Many today think there are other ways to God, as long as they believe in something greater than themselves. And then some think of Jesus as a good man, a prophet perhaps, and then create their own deity around their belief. Being sincere is not enough. Here is a story that illustrates this idea:

The three-alarm fire started in an upstairs bedroom. By the time the first responders arrived, the building was in full blaze. A young couple and their three-year-old son stood outside huddled together, all sharing a blanket.

"My baby, my baby is still in there!" the mother shouted. "She's still in her crib."

The brave fire fighter rushed into the burning building, battling the smoke and flames. Finally, he saw the infant's crib. Quickly, the man grabbed the child, wrapped it in a blanket, and prayed that he'd make it out of the house alive with the baby. Outside, the mother rushed to the fire fighter, grabbed her baby, and began to thank the man for the rescue. But then, her relief turned to horror. As she peeled back the layers of the tiny blanket, she didn't see the beautiful face of her child but saw instead the artificial features of a life-like doll that had been lying next to the infant. The fire fighter truly believed that he had picked up the child, but he had been mistaken. A classic case of being sincere but being sincerely wrong.

Sincerity and even honesty are revered in our culture. In fact, these are admirable traits in a biblical context as well. "No other faith system leads people to the one true God. Some people chafe at such an exclusive stance, but the words of Jesus and the apostles leave no other option."[1]

So, again He does not merely show the way; He *is* the way. He is not just *one* of many ways. He is the *only* Way. No one comes to the Father except through Him. That is very clear.

---

1 NIV Quest Study Bible, Copyright © 1994, 2003, 2011 by Zondervan.

## PRAYER

*Dear Lord, I recognize and affirm the fact that there is no other way to You except through Your Son, Jesus. What He did on the cross, is evidence that we can only trust You through Him.*

## DISCUSSION

1. How can we get to God? Are there other ways? Other religions?

## MORE FOOD FOR THOUGHT

1. Read Proverbs 14:12 and Matthew 7:13–14. What does this say about the right way?

## DAY 7

*If you had known Me, you would have known My Father also; from now on you know Him and have seen Him. (John 14:7)*

Can anyone actually see God? According to John 1:18, the answer is no. However, the Old Testament mentions the appearance of God to some of the faithful patriarchs.

The Lord appeared to Abraham, Moses, and Jacob but there's no mention that these men saw the actual face of the Almighty. Sometimes God's messengers (angels) were recognized as a manifestation of God that human eyes could see. There was the burning bush that appeared to Moses, but according to Exodus 3:6, "Moses hid his face, for he was afraid to look at God" Later, God tells Moses, "You cannot see my face, for mankind shall not see me and live."

However, Jesus Himself tells the disciples that He is the embodiment of God, God Incarnate. He had mentioned this before by saying that He *was* God. But as Jesus was about to die, He wanted to emphasize that these men were looking into the face of God when they looked at the rabbi they had loved and followed for three years.

Jesus got in a lot of trouble with the Pharisees by saying that He was God. One occasion was reported by Luke in his Gospel, Chapter Five (verses 17–20).

> One day He was teaching, and there were some Pharisees and teachers of the Law sitting there who had come from every village of Galilee and Judea, and from Jerusalem; and the power of the Lord was present for Him to perform healing. And some men were carrying a man on a stretcher who was paralyzed; and they were trying to bring him in and to set him down in front of Him. But when they did not find any way to

> bring him in because of the crowd, they went up on the roof and let him down through the tiles with his stretcher, into the middle of the crowd, in front of Jesus. And seeing their faith, He said, "Friend, your sins are forgiven you."

There was probably an audible gasp, and some in the crowd were incredulous that this Man would say to anyone that He could forgive sins. Only God could do that. But since Jesus was God in flesh, He had this authority. This is from where the accusations that led to His arrest and crucifixion came. His enemies heard what Jesus said about Himself and called it blasphemy.

What does this part of the farewell address mean to us today? God decided to send Himself to earth for many reasons, and just a few are: 1) to show humans what He, the invisible One, is like, 2) to preach and to teach of God's love and forgiveness 3) to give His life as a sacrifice to ransom us from the consequences of our sin.

Does this comfort you, that Jesus and God were one and the same, and that the Holy Spirit is present with us?

### PRAYER

*Oh God, I want to know you as well as it's possible. Even though I can't see you with my eyes, I know that you're with me every day.*

### DISCUSSION

1. Can we see God with our eyes?

2. Does that mean He doesn't exist?

3. Does this mean that you cannot believe in Him even though you can't see Him?

## MORE FOOD FOR THOUGHT

1. Read Matthew 5:8 about seeing God. What does this teach us?

## DAY EIGHT

*Philip said to Him, "Lord, show us the Father, and it is enough for us." Jesus said to him, "Have I been with you for so long a time, and yet you have not come to know Me, Philip? The one who has seen Me has seen the Father; how can you say, "Show us the Father"? Do you not believe that I am in the Father, and the Father is in Me? The words that I say to you I do not speak on My own, but the Father, as He remains in Me, does His works. Believe Me that I am in the Father and the Father is in Me; otherwise believe because of the works themselves. Truly, truly I say to you, the one who believes in Me, the works that I do, he will do also; and greater works than these he will do; because I am going to the Father." (John 14:8-12)*

As if He hadn't ever mentioned before that He and the Father were one, Philip revisits this concept. (Perhaps a strange question since Jesus had just gone over this?) There's no way to know whether this query made Jesus roll His eyes and shake His head and to think: *Oh boy, these guys just don't get it.* Like a parent trying to make a child obey a previous instruction, He could have responded with, "What did I just say?" But Jesus didn't miss a beat. He admonished Philip and the rest with a question: *Do you not believe?* This was a rhetorical question which seemed to silence those who heard it. Perhaps they were embarrassed or engaged in their self-doubt—soul searching, as it were. He had performed miracle after miracle in their presence. He had even given them power to perform miracles, and yet they still had doubts about who He was.

Philip's first request, "show us the Father" is followed by "...and it is enough for us." Perhaps Philip was implying that there was something missing in their lives that he believed only God could supply. When the apostle Paul asked God to take away a "thorn in the flesh" it might have been an illness, a physical condition, or even adversarial people in his life. Either way it was something that he felt was holding him back. He writes in 2 Corinthians 12:8-9, "Concerning this I pleaded with the Lord three times that it might leave me. And He has said to me, 'My grace is sufficient for you, for power is perfected in weakness.' "

The important takeaway here is that Philip recognized, even then, that he could only be complete in God.

When you face an adversary remember that "God is a safe place to hide, ready to help when we need him." (Psalm 46:1 MSG) "Nothing will be impossible with God." (Luke 1:37) "…cast all your anxiety on Him, because He cares about you." (1 Peter 5:7).

> If we find ourselves with a desire that nothing in this world can satisfy, the most probable explanation is that we were made for another world. (C.S. Lewis)

He is enough.

**PRAYER**

*Father, help me understand how I can be complete in my relationship with You. I know you care for me and so I give you all of my burdens and concerns.*

**DISCUSSION:**

1. What are you most concerned about?

2. How can you "give" Him the things that burden you?

## MORE FOOD FOR THOUGHT

1. Read Colossians 2:10; Philippians 1:6; 2 Corinthians 12:9, Philippians 4:13 about being complete in Christ.

## DAY 9

"And whatever you ask in My name, this I will do, so that the Father may be glorified in the Son. If you ask Me anything in My name, I will do it." John 14:13–14

These may be some of the most misunderstood words of Jesus recorded in the Bible. Similar promises appear in other places: Matthew 7:7–8; 21:22; Mark 11:24; Luke 11:9; and John 15:7. It is rather confusing. In fact, many nonbelievers use these passages to claim inconsistencies in scripture. And their proof is that they or someone they know asked God for something, and they did not receive it. Theologians explain this discrepancy by saying such things as "He will grant those things that align with His will and plan for the kingdom."[2]

As a believer, you may have asked for something from the Father that He did not supply the way you expected. By putting this in context with the other ask-and-receive promises, hopefully it becomes clearer. Of the Matthew passage "Ask, and it will be given to you; seek, and you will find; knock, and it will be opened to you. For everyone who asks receives, and the one who seeks finds, and to the one who knocks it will be opened…" Matthew goes on to compare it to the earthly relationship of fathers and sons.

Or what person is there among you who, when his son asks for a loaf of bread, will give him a stone? Or if he asks for a fish, he will not give him a snake, will he? So, if you, despite being evil, know how to give good gifts to your children, how much more will your Father who is in heaven give good things to those who ask Him! (Matthew 7:9–11)

---

2. John D. Barry et al., *Faithlife Study Bible* (Bellingham, WA: Lexham Press, 2012, 2016).

A parent (a good one, that is) would understand this better. Just because your child wants something (even begs for it) doesn't mean that you'll grant it. Why? Parental wisdom would not provide a child with something that could be harmful or is not useful. Our prayers are based in a relationship, as Jesus points out in Matthew 7:8. If a child asks his parents for something the father knows to be hurtful, the request is denied. The child may be frustrated and unhappy when he doesn't get what he asked for, but he must trust his father. Conversely, when the child asks for something that the father knows is beneficial, the father will provide it eagerly because he loves his child.[3]

Tony Evans writes, "Prayer is an earthly request for heavenly intervention."[4] In other words, there are two different forces at work. What God deems good and perfect; the human may not understand at all.

Timothy Keller writes, "God will either give us what we ask or give us what we would have asked if we knew everything He knows."[5]

Does this mean we should not ask unless we're sure that it is in God's ultimate will? No. Since we don't know the fullness of His will, we can't use that as a guideline. We can, however, heed the words of James (4:3) "When you ask, you do not receive, because you ask with wrong motives, that you may spend what you get on your pleasures."

Those who trust God for the right things in the right way can have confidence that God will "supply every need . . . according to his riches in glory in Christ Jesus" (Philippians 4:19).[6]

I must admit that I do not know how intercessory prayer works: praying

3. *https://www.gotquestions.org/ask-and-you-shall-receive.html.*
4. Tony Evans, "Victory in Spiritual Warfare."
5. Timothy Keller, *Prayer: Experiencing Awe and Intimacy with God* (Dutton, 2014).
6. The ESV Global Study Bible®, ESV Bible® Copyright © 2012 by Crossway. All rights reserved.

for healing or for comfort or safety for us or others. This I know, however: When we ask in His name, we are placing our total faith and trust in God's plan.

### PRAYER

*Lord, I will come to You with all of my needs, wants, and cares. I know that You hear me and that You will answer in a way that only You can.*

### DISCUSSION

1. Do you believe that God can hear you when you pray?

2. When you ask for something can you always expect God to give it to you?

3. Why or why not?

### MORE FOOD FOR THOUGHT

1. These scriptures can perhaps help you to live in God's will: Romans 12:2; Ephesians 5:17; 1 Thessalonians 5:16–18

## DAY 10

*"If you love Me, you will keep My commandments." John 14:15*

In this life, obedience isn't often associated with love. In fact, there are men, women, and children who obey their authorities out of absolute fear. Many abusive husbands, wives, fathers, mothers, leaders, and bosses try to whip their charges into shape by terrorizing them. Of course, that isn't what Jesus is talking about here. He says that love for Him cannot be separated from obedience.

It is said that true obedience is the natural outflow of a heart filled with true love. In other words, to obey God is not some difficult duty that we have. It's just the overflow of our gratitude for all that the Lord has done for us.[7]

It is hard to obey authorities you do not believe. If you voted for a certain politician, obedience to the law he or she created is not so hard. Your purpose and philosophies align for you to support him or her. It is similar with God. You love Him, believe in Him and His purpose, you appreciate all that He's done—and then obedience is born out of trust that He knows better than you about everything you need.

First John 5 says, "This is love for God that we obey his commands, and his commands are not burdensome." There's the difference—that we don't obey Him out of drudgery and obligation, but out of confidence in Him.

> It is Christ who is to be exalted, not our feelings. We will know Him by obedience, not by emotions. Our love will be shown by obedience, not by how good we feel about God at a given moment. And love means following the commands of

7. https://zume.vision/articles/love-means-obedience/.

> God. "Do you love Me?" Jesus asked Peter. "Feed My lambs." He was not asking, "How do you feel about Me?" for love is not a feeling. He was asking for action.—Elisabeth Elliot[8]

So, how does obedience to His commandments play out? When some of His critics asked Jesus what the greatest commandment was, they were referring to the Ten Commandments—and they were trying to trick Him into saying something against their legalism. But He summarized all ten by saying, "You shall love the Lord your God with all your heart, and with all your soul, and with all your mind.' This is the great and foremost commandment. The second is like it, you shall love your neighbor as yourself" (Matthew 22:37–39).

So, there is no separating love and obedience. One without the other isn't faith-based. To know Him is to love Him and to love Him is to obey Him. Get to know Him through His Word and through Spirit revelation.

### PRAYER

*Father, it is a pleasure to obey You, for I love You, and know that You would never ask something of me that You did not think was for my good.*

### DISCUSSION:

1. What is the best way to show your love for God?
2. When you say you love God, how should you treat other people?

### MORE FOOD FOR THOUGHT

1. Read Joshua 22:5; Philippians 2:8; 1 John 2:5; 2 John 1:6 if you need more motivation to obey Him out of love.

---

8. Elisabeth Elliot, *Keep a Quiet Heart* (Revell, 1995).

## DAY 11

*"I will ask the Father, and He will give you another Helper, so that He may be with you forever; the Helper is the Spirit of truth, whom the world cannot receive, because it does not see Him or know Him; but you know Him because He remains with you and will be in you." John 14:16-17*

Jesus refers to the Holy Spirit as a "helper." The Spirit of God was introduced in the first sentences of the Bible "In the beginning God created the heavens and the earth. Now the earth was formless and empty, darkness was over the surface of the deep, and the *Spirit of God* was hovering over the waters" (Genesis 1:1–2). Here God's spirit existed but only externally over His creation.

Later in scripture this "helper" is the Spirit coming *upon* an individual. However, here Jesus promises something "far from being an impersonal force, the Spirit is a person, another counselor" who takes Jesus' place when he returns to the Father; the Greek word for 'another' means one of the same kind.

Although the word "trinity" doesn't appear in scripture, the concept certainly does. And here is one place in scripture where Christ's followers learned about the three-in-one idea. In other places in scripture, the Holy Spirit is called counselor, comforter, intercessor. Each one of these words (and others) describe a different function of this part of the trinity.

As counselor, He is what Jesus called a "helper." That sounds general, if not vague. However, the psalmist uses this term in reference to Yahweh. David refers to Him as a deliverer from death or destruction. That could be a function that we can understand—a rescuer.

Two functions of the Holy Spirit (the ones I call upon the most) are *comforter* and *intercessor*. Paul tells his readers that it is He "who comforts us in all our affliction" (2 Corinthians 1:4). If you've ever been sick or despondent, you've probably called upon the Comforter for healing and/or peace in the middle of a trial. We heed the words of Paul to the Philippians, "...let your requests be made known to God. And the peace of God, which surpasses all understanding, will guard your hearts and your minds in Christ Jesus." (Philippians 4:7)

The intercessor that is the Holy Spirit is a function that I call upon when I just can't put words to my prayers. Romans 8:26 says "Now in the same way the Spirit also helps our weakness; for we do not know what to pray for as we should, but the Spirit Himself intercedes for us with groanings too deep for words..." A heart cry that I couldn't put into words is my favorite of the many purposes of the Holy Spirit. I have been so grieved that I couldn't do anything except call on the Intercessor to silently search me and give me strength.

**PRAYER:**

*God, sometimes I'm speechless before You, and I don't know how to pray. I call upon Your Spirit right now to hear my heart's cry and answer me.*

**DISCUSSION:**

1. Do I need to pray out loud? Why or why not?

2. What if I can't think of what to pray?

**MORE FOOD FOR THOUGHT**

1. Second Timothy 1:7, 1 John 4:18 and Acts 1:8 are scriptures that you might want to memorize in times when you struggle with what and how to pray.

## DAY 12

*"I will not leave you as orphans; I am coming to you." (John 14:18)*

A reference to orphans is often paired in scripture with widows. Both imply aloneness and perhaps destitution. Since women and children had no rights at the time of Jesus, without a husband or father, a woman or child was in deep dismay without someone to take care of them. We can only imagine the desperation they might feel.

Though I have not been an orphan, I have felt totally abandoned by everyone at least once in my lifetime. I was in a season of life when my faith was rocked by tragic events, and I wasn't mature enough to rely on the Father to restore me and comfort me during this time. I spent a lot of time trying to "belong." I had a horror of being alone.

I heard about a little boy who was scared one night during a powerful thunderstorm. He called out to his father from his bedroom and said, "Daddy, I'm scared. Come in here."

His dad, who had already settled in for the night, told the little boy, "Son, it's all right. God is with you in that room right now. You're OK."

There was a moment of silence. Then the little boy shot back, "Dad, right now I need someone with skin on."

"Seeing is believing" the adage goes. Because we're finite beings, we have a hard time believing in something we cannot see. After Jesus' resurrection, Thomas, had said he wouldn't believe in the resurrection without tactile proof—sight and touch. Jesus said to Thomas, "Because you have seen Me, have you now believed? Blessed are they who did not see, and yet believed." And that's us. We've seen how He has changed lives, but we haven't yet seen Him. We will, but not yet. Even if our eyes can't see Him,

I believe that God can send someone in His place to satisfy our hunger for a personal encounter with Him.

Having faith in the unknown does not imply gullibility, believing everything we see or hear without testing it alongside scripture. Colossians 2:8 says, "See to it that there is no one who takes you captive through philosophy and empty deception in accordance with human tradition, in accordance with the elementary principles of the world, rather than in accordance with Christ."

How do we stay focused, believing and following and serving, on One we have not seen? *He* stays in touch with *us* through His Word, through godly people, through speaking to us (which occasionally is audible, but mostly not) and sometimes through a direct revelation to our hearts—that still, small voice that only we can hear. It's up to us to focus and be still and listen because the unseen is real—even without skin on.

**PRAYER:**

*Father, even if I can't see You, I know you're there. I can talk to You, and I know You hear me. Help me to talk to You often even when I'm alone.*

**DISCUSSION:**

1. How can we trust God when we can't see Him?

2. Can we hear God? How?

**MORE FOOD FOR THOUGHT**

1. Matthew 28:20, Isaiah 41:10, 2 Corinthians 1:3–4 are words you can repeat whenever you feel totally alone.

## DAY 13

*After a little while, the world no longer is going to see Me, but you are going to see Me; because I live, you also will live." (John 14:18-19)*

This was a matter of life and death, literally.

At the table, I'm sure that these men were acquainted with the idea of life after death, but how that all works, I'm certain, was as confusing then as it is now.

Perhaps Jesus was trying to stress the fact that He was going away physically but He would rise from the dead. But after this event, the meaning included a broader stroke.

In Jesus' time on earth, He healed many people, and He raised some from the dead. However, the New Testament only mentions three resurrections: the son of a widow of Nain found in Luke 7, the raising of Jairus' daughter found in Mark 5:21–43, Matthew 9:18–26, and Luke 8:40–56. But the most memorable act of Jesus' resurrecting power is when He had heard that His friend Lazarus had died. (John 11).

The news first is that Lazarus is on his deathbed. His sisters send a message to Jesus who is already in Judea, not too far from Bethany where Lazarus and his sisters live. Jesus receives the message, but according to John's account of this event, He deliberately waits until Lazarus has died before He shows up at His friend's gravesite. Jesus is overcome with emotion when He sees the tomb and the distraught people. But He says, "I am the resurrection and the life; the one who believes in Me will live, even if he dies, and everyone who lives and believes in Me will never die. Do you believe this?"

I believe that, at the table, Jesus was referring to this of at least seven "I Am" statements He made.

I believe that Jesus was being emphatic in this statement. He wasn't saying that He would literally continue to raise corpses to life, but that He Himself would rise from the dead so that we all can rise to live eternally after our bodies die.

Paul picks up the topic.

"Now if we have died with Christ, we believe that we shall also live with Him, knowing that Christ, having been raised from the dead, is never to die again; death no longer is master over Him. For the death that He died, He died to sin once for all time; but the life that He lives, He lives to God. So, you too, consider yourselves to be dead to sin, but alive to God in Christ Jesus." (Romans 6:8–11)

This is the idea that to live with God we must die to ourselves first. Not physically (like Lazarus), but spiritually. This is one of those admonitions to surrender (everyday) to our fears, our doubts, and our selfishness to receive life in Him now and eternally. This is not easy to do. Dying to self seems counterintuitive, especially these days when self-awareness and self-assertiveness are being both shouted and whispered to our souls. Remember and embrace these words:

The Spirit of God, who raised Jesus from the dead, lives in you. And just as God raised Christ Jesus from the dead, he will give life to your mortal bodies by this same Spirit living within you. (Romans 6:10–11)

**PRAYER:**

*Jesus, I know that when you walked the earth, You had the power to raise people from the dead. I believe now that can make me spiritually alive even though I was dead in my sins.*

**DISCUSSION**

1. How can we be dead and brought back to life?

2. What must we do to be resurrected from our death caused by sin?

## MORE FOOD FOR THOUGHT

1. Read these passages to learn more about new life: 2 Corinthians 5:8; Philippians 1:21–2; 1 Corinthians 15:52–53

## DAY 14

*"On that day you will know that I am in My Father, and you are in Me, and I in you." (John 14:20)*

The important words in this passage are "you will know..." The same writer who penned this Gospel is the same one who wrote letters to Jews scattered over the world.

> These things I have written to you who believe in the name of the Son of God, so **that you may know** that you have eternal life. This is the **confidence** which we have before Him, that, if we ask anything according to His will, He hears us. (1 John 5:13–14, emphasis mine)

When affliction comes, it may seem that you can't bear it any longer. You might cry to God, "What have I done to deserve this?"

The story of Job in the Bible has always intrigued me. In the first chapter it says, "The Lord said to Satan, 'Have you considered My servant Job? For there is no one like him on the earth, a blameless and upright man, fearing God and turning away from evil.' "

Satan challenges God about Job's character and faithfulness. God allows the devil to test Job's devotion with trials of every kind, f9rom taking away his children, his wealth, and finally his health. After much agony and pain, the derision of his wife and the accusations from his best friends, Job finally says, "Yet as for me, I know that my Redeemer lives, And at the last, He will take His stand on the earth." (Job 19:25) Later, Job says to God, "I know that You can do all things, And that no plan is impossible for You" (Job 42:2).

That is such a story of confidence in God! Though Job didn't understand why all these horrible things were happening to him, he would not curse God.

The hymn writer Horatio Spafford was a successful 19th century lawyer in Chicago, and he had many real estate investments in the city. All of these were lost in the Great Chicago Fire of 1871. He also lost money in the economic crash of 1873. His family was devastated, and Horatio believed that a change of scenery might relieve some of their grief and stress. He booked passage on a ship to England for him, his wife, and their four daughters. Before boarding, at the last minute, Horatio had to cancel his own passage because of some business matters he had to take care of. He promised to come to his family as soon as he could.

A week into the voyage, on November 22, 1873, the ocean liner collided with a British clipper. The ship was struck, and within twelve minutes the ship sank, killing an estimated 226 people—including all four of the Spafford daughters. Anna, his wife, survived the shipwreck by clinging to a floating plank. All four daughters drowned.

When he heard the news, Horatio boarded another ship to connect with his wife in Europe. At one point during the voyage, the ship's captain summoned Horatio to his cabin and explained that he had determined the exact spot where the ship had gone down. He let Horatio know that they were at that moment passing that very spot. Horatio then returned to his own cabin and wrote his famous hymn.

"When peace like a river attendeth my way
When sorrows like sea billows roll
Whatever my lot, Thou hast taught me to say
It is well, it is well with my soul."[9]

Jesus never promised that life on earth was without trials, but He continued to reassure His disciples that they would know (be confident of these things) "on that day."

---

9. Robert J. Morgan, *Then Sings My Soul: 150 of the World's Greatest Hymn Stories* (Nashville, TN: Thomas Nelson, 2003).

## PRAYER

*Lord, I know that all things are possible with You. I am sure that You have a plan for me, and I promise that I will praise You even in the storms of life.*

## DISCUSSION

1. Do you believe that God is with you all the time?

2. How does He show You He is with you?

## MORE FOOD FOR THOUGHT

1. Titus 1:2, 2 Corinthians 5:1, Philippians 3:20–21 are words that can assure you of His presence.

## DAY 15

*The one who has My commandments and keeps them is the one who loves Me; and the one who loves Me will be loved by My Father, and I will love him and will reveal Myself to him. (John 14:21)*

In his book *Living Above the Level of Mediocrity* Charles Swindoll illustrates beautifully these words spoken at the table.

> Imagine, if you will, that you work for a company whose president found it necessary to travel out of the country and spend an extended period of time abroad. So, he says to you and the other trusted employees, "Look, I'm going to leave. And while I'm gone, I want you to pay close attention to the business. You manage things while I'm away. I will write you regularly. When I do, I will instruct you in what you should do from now until I return from this trip." Everyone agrees.
>
> He leaves and stays gone for a couple of years. During that time, he writes often, communicating his desires and concerns. Finally, he returns. He walks up to the front door of the company and immediately discovers everything is in a mess—weeds flourishing in the flower beds, windows broken across the front of the building, the [receptionist] at the front desk dozing, loud music roaring from several offices...Instead of making a profit, the business has suffered a great loss. Without hesitation he calls everyone together and with a frown asks, "What happened? Didn't you get my letters?"
>
> You say, "Oh, yeah, sure. We got all your letters. We've even bound them in a book. And some of us have memorized them. In fact, we have 'letter study' every Sunday. You know, those were really great letters." I think the president would then ask, "But what did you do about my instructions?" And, no doubt the employees would respond, "Do? Well, nothing. But we read every one!"

I believe this was what Jesus was saying here in the after-dinner speech. Many of us say we love God, and we say we read and know His word, but do we obey it to the letter? We have His commandants throughout the Bible, but when we do them, we show our love for Him.

Jesus said in the Sermon on the Mount:

> "Therefore, everyone who hears these words of Mine, and acts on them, will be like a wise man who built his house on the rock. And the rain fell, and the floods came, and the winds blew and slammed against that house; and yet it did not fall, for it had been founded on the rock. And everyone who hears these words of Mine, and does not act on them, will be like a foolish man who built his house on the sand. And the rain fell, and the floods came, and the winds blew and slammed against that house; and it fell—and its collapse was great." (Matthew 7:4-27)

### PRAYER

*Father, I pledge my time and my thoughts to You. I will make sure that my acts are in line with Your will.*

### DISCUSSION

1. Have you ever seen a building that is unstable?

2. What could have been done to make it stand strong?

### MORE FOOD FOR THOUGHT

1. These scriptures will help you stand firm on His commands: Deuteronomy 7:9, 1 Kings 8:58, Nehemiah 1:5, Daniel 9:4, 1 John 2:3.

## DAY 16

*"Judas (not Iscariot) said to Him, 'Lord, what has happened that You are going to reveal Yourself to us and not to the world?' Jesus answered and said to him, 'If anyone loves Me, he will follow My word; and My Father will love him, and We will come to him and make Our dwelling with him. The one who does not love Me does not follow My words; and the word which you hear is not Mine, but the Father's who sent Me.' " (John 14:22-24)*

John, in this writing, makes sure that the readers of his Gospel know that this Judas was not the same Judas who betrayed Jesus. This Judas is believed to be the same man as the apostle Thaddeus or sometimes even called Jude. The debate continues whether this was Jude, Jesus' brother, and/or the Jude who wrote the epistle. No one knows for certain, and that's not so important right now.

From this point on, I'll refer to him as Thaddeus.

We don't know much about Thaddeus because he isn't recorded as having said anything or done anything out of the ordinary. He must have just obeyed his teacher and gone about doing the work he was assigned.

The question that Thaddeus asks at the table is a little strange and, it seems quite off-topic. Apparently, Thaddeus, maybe others, had expected Jesus to make a public announcement or declaration of His Messiahship, but because the apostles are hidden in an upper room for the supper, maybe Thaddeus is confused. Or maybe he is even wondering why he had been chosen to be in this elite group. It seems that Thaddeus has one line of dialogue in the gospels, but that doesn't mean that he was not a devoted disciple. Having seen Jesus perform many miracles, he was probably taking it all in to be able to be a strong influence in the kingdom of God.

Jesus would later tell His men in this same address, "You did not choose Me, but I chose you, and appointed you that you would go and bear fruit..."

We have been chosen. Set aside for His work. But often we wonder why. We're flawed and naïve. We may never have our names written up in theological journals or even be praised publicly for our work. In fact, our love for Him and service to Him should not be tied to expectations for reward.

> "For you see your calling, brethren, that not many wise according to the flesh, not many mighty, not many noble, are called."[10]

It is obvious that Jesus did not call all His disciples to full-time ministry while He was still on earth, for, though the men followed Him, they continued to fish and mend nets to make a living.

Every believer is called to ministry: doctors, teachers, stay-at-home moms and dads, construction workers.

For you have been called for this purpose, because Christ also suffered for you, leaving you an example, so that you would follow in His steps… (1 Peter 2:21)

**PRAYER:**

*Thank you, Father, for choosing me to be one of Your children. Because You are my Father, I love You and trust You.*

**DISCUSSION:**

1. How do you know that you are one of His children?

2. Because He chose you, what must you do for Him?

10. John F. MacArthur, *Twelve Ordinary Men* Kindle Edition (Nashville, TN: Thomas Nelson).

3. What does it mean to follow in His steps?

## MORE FOOD FOR THOUGHT

1. In 1 Peter 2:9, what does it say about who we are in Christ? How will this idea change you?

## DAY 17

*"These things I have spoken to you while remaining with you. But the Helper, the Holy Spirit whom the Father will send in My name, He will teach you all things, and remind you of all that I said to you." (John 14:25-26)*

So much to learn. So little time.

Three years with the Master wasn't long enough for the disciples to learn everything Jesus wanted to teach them. He knew that their knowledge and understanding would have to be an ongoing process. That's why He reassures His men that after He's gone, He will send a Helper (Holy Spirit) to **1)** teach them all things and to **2)** remind them what they had already learned.

It seems that the Holy Spirit has several functions, and commentators vary on their view of how many. But these two Jesus chose to highlight in this passage.

Mrs. Woodham was my second-grade teacher. She was kind and would answer even the most childish questions. She was smart and knew how to teach her second graders the things they needed to know from the textbook and other sources. And when we disobeyed direct orders, she disciplined us. (I stood in the corner several times that year.) I trusted her instruction, and I loved her dearly. It was the only year in school that I had perfect attendance. I didn't want to miss a day with her.

I think Jesus knew this was the kind of teacher He would send when He said these words. The Helper's teaching can come from direct revelation (one-on-one), from the printed Word, and from even bad choices that we make. Christian apologist Josh McDowell writes about the Holy Spirit, "Some people believe that the Holy Spirit is the influence of good—like the 'good force of the universe.' But the Holy Spirit is a person—the third person of the Trinity."[11] We as students need to trust Him because He knows the textbook, and He lets us learn through our bad choices. He reminds us of things He's already taught us, and sometimes we must stand in the corner to get the message.

*The Message* puts this passage like this:

> The Friend, the Holy Spirit whom the Father will send at my request, will make everything plain to you.

Don't miss a day with this teacher. Listen to His teachings and take your punishment when you disobey.

**PRAYER:**

*Teach me, O Lord. I am ready to learn. I will listen to You and absorb all the lessons You have for me.*

**DISCUSSION:**

1. Who is your favorite teacher?

2. What have you learned from that teacher?

11. Josh and Sean McDowell, *77 FAQs about God and the Bible* (Eugene, OR: Harvest House, 2012).

3. Are you ready to be taught more?

## MORE FOOD FOR THOUGHT

1. Many writers of the Psalms ask God to teach them. Here are a few scriptures to read as you pray that the Lord will teach you His ways: Psalm 25:4–5; Psalm 32:8; Psalm 86:11; Psalm 119:33; Psalm 119:66

## DAY 18

*Peace I leave you, My peace I give you; not as the world gives, do I give to you. Do not let your hearts be troubled, nor fearful. (John 14:27)*

This is one of my favorite lines in this speech. It's also one that perhaps all other people in that Upper Room had experienced, like when Jesus calmed the Sea of Galilee during a storm.

However, I don't think this kind of peace describes what Jesus meant here. This whole speech is a bit of a last will and testament. He knew He was leaving, and He bequeathed His disciples the thing of most value to their lives. "Peace I leave you. My peace." He repeats it with the emphatic "My," and says that this is an actual possession that only He can give them. What is *His* peace? That is a deep topic, and it has many parts.

The first part is making peace *with* God.

Romans 5:1–2: "Therefore, having been justified by faith, we have peace with God through our Lord Jesus Christ..."

Here's the first step. We became His enemies because of our sin. "Once you were alienated from God and were enemies in your minds because of your evil behavior." Colossians 1:21

Evil might sound like a harsh word for our deeds. We associate Satan with evil, and we try to categorize the transgressions of man in their degrees of evil. But Paul writes (Romans 3:23) "...all have sinned and fall short of the glory of God." This is where peace starts: settling with a perfect God by admitting our imperfections.

Then there's the peace *of* God—inner peace. Paul, again, puts it this way:

> Do not be anxious about anything, but in everything by prayer and pleading with thanksgiving let your requests be

> made known to God. And the peace of God, which surpasses all comprehension, will guard your hearts and minds in Christ Jesus." (Philippians 4:7)

Finally, there's peace between people. In Romans 12:18, Paul writes, "If it is possible, as far as it depends on you, live at peace with everyone." I believe this kind of peace is a byproduct of the other two steps. Peace *with* God and the peace *of* God. This calls us to make peace with others as much as we can.

> "Life with God is not immunity from difficulties, but peace in difficulties." (C. S. Lewis)

A few years ago, my husband and I visited Mamertine Prison in Rome, Italy. This was assumed to be the last place that Simon Peter and Paul were held before their executions by Nero. It was a dark, damp dungeon—accessed through a small hole in the floor. Prisoners either starved to death there or were lifted out to be executed. One of Peter's last writings was a letter to the universal church. He writes: "...be diligent to be found by Him in peace, spotless and blameless...but grow in the grace and knowledge of our Lord and Savior Jesus Christ. To him be the glory both now and to the day of eternity. Amen" (2 Peter 3:18).

Paul's final written words were:

> The Lord will rescue me from every evil deed and bring me safely into his heavenly kingdom. To him be the glory forever and ever. Amen. (2 Timothy 4:18)

These words don't sound like men who are conflicted or afraid of what was about to happen to them. They were men who had that peace that passes comprehension.

Pray specifically for that kind of peace, especially in the middle of the storms of life. It is part of your inheritance.

## PRAYER:

*Jesus, just like You calmed the storms around the disciples, please help me to trust You to do the same thing for me. I know that trouble will come but help me through these hard times.*

## DISCUSSION

1. What was the latest "storm" you were in?

2. How did God give you peace in the middle of that storm?

3. Can God help you stay calm when life is unpleasant?

## MORE FOOD FOR THOUGHT

1. Read Isaiah 26, the whole chapter. Much of this was written to Israelis in that day but read it as if God is speaking to you about peace.

## DAY 19

*"You heard that I said to you, 'I am going away, and I am coming to you.' If you loved Me, you would have* rejoiced *because I am going to the Father, for the Father is greater than I. And now I told you before it happens, so that when it happens, you may believe." (John 14:28-29)*

"Rejoice" is not a word we use often in everyday language, but it can be found all over the Bible. The meaning of the word is "an action that comes out of a heart full of gratitude. It implies exuberance as in the excitement of a sports fan when his or her team scores. It even means to boast, which would follow the sports fan comparison."[12] The word "joy" is the root of this word.

Jesus uses this in a different way than we usually think, however. He uses it as a condition for love. "If you loved…would have rejoiced." Why? They all knew He would be leaving soon. Only *He* knew He would die a horrible death and then rise from the dead on the third day.

It sounds like Jesus is chiding His men for not rejoicing when they realized He was going away. Grief would come to them all too soon. Was He questioning their love for Him since they knew He would be leaving?

Can grief and joy coexist in a person's life? That depends on your definition of joy. The *Merriam-Webster Dictionary* defines it as: "the emotion evoked by well-being, success, or good fortune or by the prospect of possessing what one desires." The Oxford dictionary defines it as "a feeling of great pleasure and happiness." Both of these have to do with feelings. But what happens when you grieve? The death of a loved one? The pain of having a prodigal child?

---

12. Tony Evans, T*he Tony Evans Bible Commentary* (Nashville, TN: Holman Bible Publishers, 2019).

Warren Wiersbe defines biblical joy as "that inward peace and sufficiency that is not affected by outward circumstances." Paul understood this definition as well as anyone. He was beaten, shipwrecked, imprisoned, and more, he still had joy. He called it "being full of sorrow and yet rejoicing" (2 Corinthians 6:10) and said in 2 Corinthians 7:4 "in all our affliction, I am overflowing with joy."

Charles Spurgeon wrote,

> *...believers are not dependent upon circumstances. Their joy comes not from what* they *have, but from what they are, not from where they are, but from whose they are,* not *from what they enjoy, but from that which was suffered for them by their Lord.*

It is like peace that passes understanding. You can't really describe joy, but you can experience it just the same.

James 1:2–3 says, "Consider it all joy, my brothers and sisters, when you encounter various trials, knowing that the testing of your faith produces endurance..."

When you feel like your sense of joy is in jeopardy remember these words from Psalms 34:18; 147:3.

The Lord is close to the brokenhearted and saves those who are crushed in spirit.

He heals the brokenhearted and binds up their wounds.

**PRAYER:**

*Lord, I know You feel pain when I am brokenhearted. I ask that You let me feel the joy of Your presence when I am sad.*

## DISCUSSION

1. When do you feel sad?

2. What do you do when you are sad?

3. Can you have joy even in sadness?

## MORE FOOD FOR THOUGHT

1. We know the story of Job and his suffering. Read chapter 19 of the Book of Job. Pay attention to verses 25 and 26. Is it possible to praise God in the middle of distress?

## DAY 20

*"I will not speak much more with you, for the ruler of the world is coming, and he has nothing in regard to Me, but so that the world may know that I love the Father, I do exactly as the Father commanded Me." (John 14:30-31)*

When He says the ruler of the world is coming, whom does He mean? Most believe that He is referring to Satan. I personally don't want to give Satan any more of my time by writing about who he is, but to know how to handle him, we need to know a little about him and his tactics. John MacArthur writes:

> [In football] one of the things that we always did was to take the third or fourth string—and this is generally how a lot of people spend their whole football career, if they play a lot of third string or fourth string football—take that unit, and make that unit look, and act, and play like the team we were going to play on Saturday. And then we would practice against our own guys, doing what our opponent was going to do, in order that we might better know the enemy. Being able to predict what your opponent is going to do is very important.[13]

Jesus knew his opponent well. He spent forty days in the wilderness with him. Here, in this speech, the Lord is making sure that His disciples know what they would be up against.

The enemy's goal on earth is implied in some of these names:

Tempter, Prince of Demons, Beelzebub, The Accuser, Father of Lies, Murderer, Prince and Power of the Air.

As the Tempter in the wilderness, Satan appealed to Jesus' human side: hunger. He offered Jesus command over the world—something that was not his to give. He even had the audacity to quote scripture from Psalm 91 to Jesus. "He will give His angels orders concerning You'; and 'On their

---

13. John F. Macarthur. *Twelve Ordinary Men.*

hands they will lift You up, So that You do not strike Your foot against a stone.'" Sounds convincing and even credible when you add a scripture reference.

Jesus knew that the disciples' road would not be easy. As hard as He worked to make Himself known, Satan was working just as hard to quash that plan.

It's a battle. Warfare. James writes in chapter 4, verse 7 of his epistle, "Resist the devil and he will flee from you."

Peter's first epistle says that Satan is like a roaring lion, "He goes around... seeking whom he may devour." Peter uses simile here to make his readers realize how dangerous and persistent he is.

Paul comes up with another metaphor for this battle—a way to fight it. He writes,

> Put on the whole armor of God, that you may be able to stand against the schemes of the devil. For we do not wrestle against flesh and blood, but against the rulers, against the authorities, against the cosmic powers over this present darkness, against the spiritual forces of evil in the heavenly places. Therefore, take up the whole armor of God, that you may be able to withstand in the evil day, and having done all, to stand firm (Ephesians 6:11–13).

**PRAYER:**

*Lord, please protect me from the lies of the devil. I'm fully trusting in You.*

**DISCUSSION:**

1. How can you tell the difference between hearing God's voice over Satan's?

2. Who is the real enemy of the believer?

## MORE FOOD FOR THOUGHT

1. Read Matthew 4:1–11, the account of Jesus being tempted in the wilderness. What devices does Satan use here?

## DAY 21

*Get up, let's go from here. (John 14:31b)*

Obviously, this is not a point of intense inspiration, or is it? After this statement at the table, Jesus led His disciples out into the Garden of Gethsemane—a garden that sits at the base of the Mount of Olives. On the way, which was perhaps a mile from the Upper Room, He finished His farewell speech to them and then had a heart-to-heart with His Father.

The men at the table that night had followed their Rabbi for three years and had seen His miracles and heard His teaching. They were willing to follow Him from the table to the garden only to witness His arrest. It seemed to be a tragic end to a glorious life. Most of the disciples scattered. Peter watched from a distance and denied publicly any connection with Him, not once, but three times. How could these faithful followers fail Him so miserably at His greatest moment of need?

In 1956, Elisabeth Elliot and her husband, Jim, were part of a missionary effort to the tribe called the Aucas who lived in the remote jungles of Ecuador. Though the missionaries believed they had made friendly contact with the tribesmen, warriors speared Jim and the other men to death. Devasted, but not deterred, Elisabeth and their daughter returned later to the very tribe that had killed her husband. Elliot heeded the call to follow Jesus and, as a result, brought salvation to this tribe.

Elisabeth wrote:

> What matters in life is that we should stick with the Lord. Where He goes, we follow. When He says halt, we halt. This is how it was with Israel—as He led them all those years in the wilderness of their journey to the Promised Land, they moved when the pillar of cloud and fire moved, and they camped when it stood still. The most amazing thing about that story is the most amazing thing about ours—the Lord of Hosts is with

> us! The pillar of cloud, visible by day, had fire in it at night, so the Israelites could see it at every stage of their journey.[14]

Obviously, there may be a cost to follow Jesus. The lyrics to the song "I Have Decided to Follow Jesus" is said to have originated from Nokseng, an India native who converted to Christianity in the middle of the 19th century and was killed, along with his family, because of his faith.

I have decided to follow Jesus;
I have decided to follow Jesus;
I have decided to follow Jesus;
No turning back; no turning back.

On their way to the garden, apparently Jesus continued His treatise.

### PRAYER:

*Father, I will follow You even when the path is not clear. I am so thankful that You have asked me to follow.*

### DISCUSSION:

1. How can you follow Jesus?

2. What must you do to follow Him?

### MORE FOOD FOR THOUGHT

1. Read Matthew 4; Matthew 16; Luke 5.

---

14. https://elisabethelliot.org/resource-library/devotionals/at-every-stage-of-the-journey/

## DAY 22

*I am the true vine, and My Father is the vinedresser. Every branch in Me that does not bear fruit, He takes away; and every branch that bears fruit, He prunes it so that it may bear more fruit. (John 15:1-2)*

In Jesus' time, many people He encountered made their living in fishing, raising sheep, or some other agricultural career path. Jesus often used metaphors from this agrarian culture to illustrate His lessons. Grape vineyards were big components of the food production of the world, so everyone knew about how and where they grew. In the Gospels alone there are over twenty references to vines and vineyards.

What does Jesus mean when He speaks of this growing process?

Later on in this same chapter, He refers to vineyards and branches. But here He identifies Himself and His Father and their roles in this metaphor.

First, He calls Himself the "true vine." This might have taken the disciples by surprise. For years, in the Old Testament, the nation of Israel was called "the vine." Isaiah, Jeremiah, the psalmists, and others compared the Jewish nation to a vine. He was telling the men of a paradigm shift on the horizon. From this point on, He would be the "true vine." No longer would it be appropriate for Israel to think that just because they are Jews, they would be a part of God's kingdom. This idea would be a game-changer.

Second, He calls the Father the vinedresser. The vinedresser was the caretaker of the vineyard. His job was to plant, prune, and tend the grapes. I believe that Jesus was identifying the Father as not only the Creator, but the Sustainer.

The vinedresser cares for the vines, tending to them, pruning them and making sure they have everything they need to flourish. What happens when the keeper of the vineyard does not maintain the plants? Weeds grow up, fruit does not mature, pests will feed on the plants and the fruit. The dresser makes sure that the vineyard is fenced and guarded so that scavengers cannot raid the vines.

Some of our American forefathers were Deists: Washington, Jefferson, Franklin, Madison, and Monroe, to name a few. A Deist believes in God as Creator, but not as one who acts to influence events. In other words, He steps back and does nothing to sustain us.

In this passage, Jesus sets the record straight. As the vinedresser, He maintains what He's planted.

He did not create us just to leave us helpless. Perhaps you're doing well now, but eventually you'll need His protection, His careful eye, and, yes, some pruning.

Cast your burden upon the Lord and He will sustain you;
He will never allow the righteous to be shaken. (Psalm 55:22)

**PRAYER:**

*God, I want to stay closely connected to the vine. Thank You for keeping me pruned and ready to do Your work.*

**DISCUSSION:**

1. What does God want us to do?

2. How can we stay connected to Him?

## DAY 23

*You are already clean because of the word which I have spoken to you.* Remain *in Me, and I in you. Just as the branch cannot bear fruit of itself but must remain in the vine, so neither can you unless you* remain *in Me. I am the vine, you are the branches; the one who* remain *in Me, and I in him bears much fruit, for apart from Me you can do nothing. If anyone does not* remain *in Me, he is thrown away like a branch and dries up; and they gather them and throw them into the fire, and they are burned. If you* remain *in Me, and My words* remain *in you, ask whatever you wish, and it will be done for you. My Father is glorified by this, that you bear much fruit, and so prove to be My disciples. (John 15:3-8)*

Continuing His agriculture metaphor, Jesus again identifies Himself as the vine, but now He says that the disciples are the branches. And He speaks of fruit now, too.

In scripture, fruit is referred to many times. Early on in the creation narrative, fruit is used to tempt Adam and Eve to sin. It is also a symbol of prosperity in the Promised Land and often given as gifts to express appreciation and honor.

However, the best use of the word "fruit" in the Bible is used allegorically by Paul the apostle. I believe that Jesus was referring to this use to illustrate what the spirit of God can produce in our lives. In Galatians 5:22–23 we'll find the fruit of the spirit listed here: "...the fruit of the Spirit is love, joy, peace, patience, kindness, goodness, faithfulness, gentleness, self-control..."

Although there are nine virtues listed, they are referred to as singular—fruit, implying that these gifts are all-or-none in the believer. You can't have one without the others. Individually, however, they have unique functions.

Love is the willing, sacrificial giving of oneself for the benefit of another without thought of return. Joy is the gladness of heart that circumstances cannot stifle. Peace is tranquility of mind, freeing one from worry and fear. Patience is the opposite of a short temper, a disposition quietly barring intolerance. Gentleness is kindness and tender treatment of others. Goodness is liberal generosity. Faithfulness here is dependability and loyalty. Self-control is restraint—the opposite of self-indulgence.

These virtues cannot be acquired through discipline or resolve to do better. This fruit grows naturally when we stay (remain) attached to Jesus. How do we do that? The same way we stay in touch with another person. Talk often. Listen even more. Learn everything you can about that person.

"The steadfast of mind You will keep in perfect peace,

Because he trusts in You." (Isaiah 26:3)

**PRAYER:**

*Jesus, I surrender to You and want so much to bear the fruit of the Spirit. Help me to want to be more like You.*

**DISCUSSION:**

1. What is the fruit of the spirit?

2. Can you have one without the others?

**MORE FOOD FOR THOUGHT**

1. Read Galatians 6:7–8; 2 Corinthians 9:6. What message is this for believers?

## DAY 24

> *"Just as the Father has loved Me, I also have loved you; remain in My love. If you keep My commandments, you will remain in My love; just as have kept My Father's commandments and remain in His love." (John 15:9-10)*

Will we ever understand love? We throw around the word "love" and even the concept so often that the word has become diluted. What happens if we dilute something? It reduces the power of the original solution.

I believe Jesus is trying to express these sentiments when telling His disciples that they should love God as He loved them. So, let's explore this kind of love Jesus is talking about without throwing out meaningless cliches.

First of all, God's love for us is called *extravagant* (2 Corinthians 13:14 MSG).

It is called unfailing and priceless (Psalms 36:7).

It is wide, long, high, and deep (Ephesians 3:18).

It surpasses knowledge (Lamentations 3:22).

How does He express His love to us? He sent His Son to die for us (Romans 5:8).

He allows us to be His children (1 John 3:1).

Now that is just the tip of the iceberg, but Jesus tells them (and us) that we should love God as He loved us. And how is that?

The "Love Chapter" referred to often is from 1 Corinthians 13. It's a favorite at weddings, of course, because it has so much to say about true love for one another.

*The Message* paraphrases this beautiful passage from verse 7:

Love never gives up.
Love cares more for others than for self.
Love doesn't want what it doesn't have.
Love doesn't strut,
Doesn't have a swelled head,
Doesn't force itself on others,
Isn't always "me first,"
Doesn't fly off the handle,
Doesn't keep score of the sins of others,
Doesn't revel when others grovel,
Takes pleasure in the flowering of truth,
Puts up with anything,
Trusts God always,
Always looks for the best,
Never looks back,
But keeps going to the end.

In His farewell address, Jesus teaches about love—His Father's for them, His for them, them for others. It must be important if He mentions it so often. Don't dilute the meaning by being careless with the definition or the expression of it. Take it seriously. He did.

**PRAYER:**

*Lord, I love You so much and I know You love me. Help me to love others the way You love me.*

**DISCUSSION:**

1. How should we love others?

2. Do we love just those who love us?

## MORE FOOD FOR THOUGHT

1. Read Romans 5:8 and 1 John 3:1. What does this say about God's love for us?

## DAY 25

*These things I have spoken to you so that My joy may be in you, and that your joy may be made full. (John 15:11)*

Joy. How can we define it? And how can our joy be made full, as Jesus says?

First, the dictionary definition of this tiny word that has great impact is: "feeling great delight with present or expected good." Feelings. Delight. Good.

Josh McDowell writes, "…some of us think we can't have joy if we're not feeling happy."[15]

It was one of many times the Jews were oppressed and living in exile. There was a Hebrew named Nehemiah who was in service to the Persian king. The king agreed to let Nehemiah and others return to Jerusalem to help rebuild the temple and the city wall that had fallen into disrepair. The rebuilders met with much opposition from the ungodly inhabitants of the area. Despite the trials of this project, the prophet Nehemiah said to them: "…the joy of the Lord is your strength" (Nehemiah 8:10).

How can one who had been in captivity and oppressed for many years speak positively about joy? Clarence L. Haynes, Jr. writes for crosswalk.com and he has redefined the definition of joy that I love.

> …an internal reservoir or well that bubbles up inside you eventually expressing itself in shouts of song, praise, and great delight.
>
> Happiness is because of. Joy is in spite of. Happiness comes as a result of the things that are happening in your life. When things are happy and good then that produces happiness. This comes from outside and works its way in. Joy on the other hand comes in spite of. While the things happening around

15. Josh McDowell, *Lecture and Teaching on Christian Joy*.

> you can in fact produce joy, your joy is not dependent on those things. Because joy flows from the reservoir inside of you; it has the ability to sustain you even if nothing on the outside gives you a reason to rejoice. This is why you can have joy in the midst of trials, hardships, or even some of the difficult places in life because it is springing up from what is inside...[16]

Look at James 1:2–4: "Consider it all joy, my brothers and sisters, when you encounter various trials, knowing that the testing of your faith produces endurance. And let endurance have its perfect result, so that you may be perfect and complete, lacking in nothing."

It's possible to have deep-down joy without having to go through horrible trials, but I believe that Haynes and James are saying that joy can be real in every circumstance—even in the middle of life's greatest sorrows and bitterest struggles.

**PRAYER:**

*Father, I choose joy. Help me to see Your hand in the middle of my struggles and stand joyfully through them.*

**DISCUSSION:**

1. Where does joy come from?

2. How can you have joy in the middle of sad times?

16. https://www.crosswalk.com/faith/spiritual-life/what-does-it-mean-to-have-true-joy.html.

## MORE FOOD FOR THOUGHT

3. In Psalm 30, David thanks God for deliverance, and in verse 5, what does he say about God's restoration of joy?

## DAY 26

*This is My commandment, that you love one another, just as I have loved you. Greater love has no one than this, that a person will lay down his life for his friends. You are My friends if you do what I command you. (John 15:12-14)*

Does this define true friendship? It seems to deviate from what we have often believed that the word "friend" is supposed to mean. According to these three sentences, friendship comes with strings attached. "You are My friends if you do what I command you." But what about unconditional love?

I don't believe that Jesus is saying that He'll call us friends until we disobey, and then He would quit loving us. There are so many places in scripture that seem to contradict this thought. So, what could it mean?

Jesus' connection with love and obedience is not new. He has linked these two concepts before even in this His Farewell Discourse (Last Supper address) and in other instances. These statements are almost too deep to imagine, mostly because earlier He speaks of the love that He wants them to have for Him. Here He is connecting the mutual relationship. Him and them. This is part of the covenant bond.

A covenant is defined as "a relationship between two partners who make binding promises to each other and work together to reach a common goal."[17]

The godly biblical covenants are everywhere in scripture, and each takes on different qualities depending on the parties involved.

First, there were covenants between God with man. Even though Abram was promised to be the father of many nations, he and his wife were barren for many years, well after they were beyond child-bearing age. But even though Abram and Sarai took matters into their own hands by decid-

17. Tony Evans, *The Tony Evans Bible Commentary*.

ing that Abram should procreate with another woman, God held up His part of the bargain even though Abram didn't.

Second, there were covenants between two people (David and Jonathan, for instance). Even the best of friends can break those covenants. That's why here in John 15, Jesus places a high value on giving one's life for another.

But more than that, He predicts His own sacrificial death to let the disciples know that His death would not be in vain. In fact, it was necessary for them (and us) to gain eternal life through this once-and-for-all act.

So, love is NOT conditional. Neither is friendship. The New Covenant that would be inaugurated with His upcoming death was dependent on the promise God made to redeem His people. The other side of the covenant is our accepting the necessary closure to this eternal, unbreakable, contract. There was no other way to fulfill this promise.

### PRAYER

*Oh God. I see your promise unfold as You sent your Son to be Your way of showing me unconditional love and friendship. I accept the pledge and close the circle that guarantees my life in heaven with You.*

### DISCUSSION

1. What does it mean to be a friend of God?

2. Will God always love you?

### MORE FOOD FOR THOUGHT

1. Read Luke 5. What are the signs of true friendship in this passage?

## DAY 27

*No longer do I call you slaves, for the slave does not know what his master is doing; but I have called you friends, because all things that I have heard from My Father I have made known to you. (John 15:15)*

It would be easy to get caught up on the implications of slavery (or servitude) juxtaposed with the idea of former slaves now being regarded as friends. But I don't think the slavery implications are pertinent here. I do believe Jesus had been talking about love for the Father, love for Him, and love for each other. This is just another way of illustrating a before-and-after scenario. We are estranged from God because of our sin, and then we become part of a family because of our adoption by Him with full benefits of a child (or a close, trusted friend). Someone not in the inner sanctum (family and friend) isn't usually told intimate plans. But the transition from alien, foreigner, outsider to heir or child of God is something that we cherish now, and that is because we probably need to be reminded of it long after this speech happened. John in one of his letters writes...

> See how great a love the Father has bestowed on us, that we would be called children of God; and such we are. For this reason, the world does not know us, because it did not know Him. Beloved, now we are children of God... (1 John 3:1–2)

Paul echoes this in his letter to the Galatians:

> Therefore, you are no longer a slave, but a son; and if a son, then an heir through God. (Galatians 4:7)

Charles Stanley writes, "If we were merely God's servants, He would just give us orders. However, Jesus wants us to build a relationship with Him as His friends—loving and fellowshipping with Him and knowing His heart."

The takeaway at the table here is that Jesus is spelling out for His disciples how much He loved them and how they should love each other.

There is a quote from Mother Teresa. (It later inspired a lyric for a song called "Anyway" by Martina McBride.)

People are unreasonable, illogical, and self-centered;
LOVE THEM ANYWAY.
If you do good, people will accuse you of selfish, ulterior motives; DO GOOD ANYWAY.
If you are successful, you win false friends and true enemies;
SUCCEED ANYWAY.
The good you do will be forgotten tomorrow;
DO GOOD ANYWAY.
Honesty and frankness make you vulnerable;
BE HONEST AND FRANK ANYWAY.
What you spent years building may be destroyed overnight;
BUILD ANYWAY.
People really need help but may attack you if you help them; HELP PEOPLE ANYWAY
Give the world the best you have and you'll get kicked in the teeth;
GIVE THE WORLD THE BEST YOU'VE GOT ANYWAY.

**PRAYER:**

*God, You saw my sin and loved and died for me anyway. Help me to love others like that.*

**DISCUSSION:**

1. How do you know that God loves you?

2. How should you react when someone is unkind or hurtful toward you?

## MORE FOOD FOR THOUGHT

1. Read Ephesians 6:5–9 and Luke 6:31 and compare the message to slaves versus the message to friends.

## DAY 28

*You did not choose Me, but I chose you, and appointed you that you would go and bear fruit, and that your fruit would remain, so that whatever you ask of the Father in My name He may give to you. This I command you, that you love one another. (John 15:16-17)*

I was almost always the last picked for the volleyball team. Being just over 5 feet tall, I was rarely selected for any athletic activity that required height. I would try hard and wish to be one of the choice players, but heredity had a different plan.

When Jesus tells His disciples that day that He had chosen them, He didn't just mean that these men were lucky to be part of an elite group that He had tapped on the shoulder before asking them to join His "band of brothers." No, I believe this was one of those times when He was also talking to me 2,000-plus years later.

First, God set apart certain people groups, the Jews, to be His own.

"The Lord your God has chosen you out of all the peoples on the face of the earth to be his people, his treasured possession" (Deuteronomy 7:6). I am not Jewish, so it would be easy to say that this idea doesn't apply to me.

However, Simon Peter writes an open letter to all believers, many Jews and Gentiles. That does include me. He writes "...you are A CHOSEN PEOPLE, A royal PRIESTHOOD, A HOLY NATION, A PEOPLE FOR *GOD'S* OWN POSSESSION," (1 Peter 2:9). I do not believe that I am an accident, all 5' foot 1" of me. I may not make the volleyball team, but I'm part of a better, eternal team.

Peter also calls us a royal priesthood. That may not mean much to me since I have neither regal roots, nor a degree from seminary. What I do have is direct access to the Holy of Holies. When Jesus breathed His last on the cross, the veil in the temple in Jerusalem was torn in two from top to bottom, taking away the barrier between mere mortals and Almighty God. We now have direct access to God. We don't have to have an anointed reverend to intercede for us anymore.

I live in a country of ungodly people, so calling me part of a holy nation has nothing to do with my physical citizenship. In fact, I am part of a new nation made up of diversity—many ethnicities, many sizes and shapes, which has no height requirement. My citizenship is in a new place called heaven.

Finally, Peter speaks of a "people for his own possession." I am possessed. Not like on scary shows where souls occupy dead bodies, but like a spirit—the Holy Spirit—that has taken over my soul, mind, and body.

I am selected not by my abilities, my characteristics, or even my works. And I didn't choose Him, but He chose me.

**PRAYER:**

*Lord, I don't know why, but You chose me to be one of Your children. Help me live up to Your holy name.*

**DISCUSSION:**

1. What does it mean to be chosen by God?

2. How can you live up to the calling?

**MORE FOOD FOR THOUGHT**

1. Psalm 33:12 and Ephesians 1:4–5 emphasize the importance of knowing that we have been chosen by God.

## DAY 29

*"If the world hates you, you know that it has hated Me before it hated you. If you were of the world, the world would love you as its own; but because you are not of the world, but I chose you out of the world, because of this the world hates you." John 15:18-19*

Hate is a strong word. Maybe you were disciplined as a child if you said it, especially if you shouted it out in anger at someone. So why would Jesus bring this up now? He had just said that He would send the Holy Spirit to comfort us and teach us and then Jesus says that we will be hated because of our faith in Him. Which is it?

Jesus introduced the idea that "the world" is made up of unbelieving people. Because we are quite distinct from all who are in rebellion against God, and we shouldn't be surprised when we become persecuted, laughed at, or maybe even abused by those who want no part of the things of God.

Because being in God's family requires surrender, this may be the greatest point of contention for many. We don't want to give up bad habits, bad attitudes, or our hopes and desires. We do not want to give up our power or authority of our own destinies.

Jesus adds in these verses, "[I]chose you out of the world" to set us apart from the rest of mankind. Does that mean that we are elite? Does it mean we are special? Yes and no. To be chosen is to be "selected or marked for favor or special privilege," according to Merriam-Webster. But there are places in other scriptures where we are "called." "...you are A CHOSEN PEOPLE, A royal PRIESTHOOD, A HOLY NATION, A PEOPLE FOR *GOD'S* OWN POSSESSION, so that you may proclaim the excellencies of Him who has called you out of darkness into His marvelous light" (1 Peter 2:9). Called and chosen. Is there a difference? To be called is to be invited. To be chosen is the next step. Accepting the invitation is a mutual decision between us and God. We are all called, but many reject or ignore the invite. But those of us who are invited, happily accept the offer. So, when Jesus makes this statement, He probably meant He called these men who were willing to come along and follow Him—most not knowing what to expect. Then they became His chosen ones.

To be chosen should never give us a sense of pride. Just the opposite. It should instill a sense of humility. Yes, *we* accepted the invitation, but He *sent* the invitation.

I am constantly amazed that He allowed me to hear the gospel early in my life and to have the foundation and the conviction to accept it. Being chosen by God, I know, is what I cherish more than anything. But that choice does not give me reason to boast. In fact, it comes with a great responsibility. Paul writes in Colossians 3:12, "Therefore, as God's chosen people, holy and dearly loved, clothe yourselves with compassion, kindness, humility, gentleness and patience."

**PRAYER:**

*Lord, I thank You for calling me. I thank You for choosing me. Let me never forget who I am: clothed with Your compassion, kindness, humility, gentleness and patience.*

**DISCUSSION:**

1. Is there a difference between being called and being chosen?

2. If so, what is it?

3. What does an RSVP mean? How does this relate to Jesus' call to us?

## MORE FOOD FOR THOUGHT

1. Read Galatians 1:10, Romans 12:2, and 1 John 3:13. What do these verses teach us about being believers in an unbelieving world?

## DAY 30

*Remember the word that I said to you, 'A slave is not greater than his master.' If they persecuted Me, they will persecute you as well; if they followed My word, they will follow yours also. But all these things they will do to you on account of My name, because they do not know the One who sent Me. If I had not come and spoken to them, they would not have sin; but now they have no excuse for their sin. The one who hates Me hates My Father also. If I had not done among them the works which no one else did, they would not have sin; but now they have both seen and hated Me and My Father as well. But this has happened so that the word that is written in their Law will be fulfilled: 'They hated Me for no reason.' (John 15:20-25)*

This is one place in this address where Jesus repeats Himself, but He also adds something new here at the table. He reiterates the slave and master relationship and the theme of hatred for Him and us shown by those outside the kingdom. But speaking of those outsiders, He says, "they have no excuse for their sin" (emphasis added). The sin He talks about is the ultimate sin of rejecting God's plan revealed through His Son.

The Parable of the Great Banquet (found in Luke 14:16–20) is a good example of this thought:

> A certain man was preparing a great banquet and invited many guests. At the time of the banquet, he sent his servant to tell those who had been invited, "Come, for everything is now ready." But they all alike began to make excuses. The first said, "I have just bought a field, and I must go and see it. Please excuse me." Another said, "I have just bought five yokes of oxen, and I'm on my way to try them out. Please excuse me." Still another said, "I just got married, so I can't come."

D.L. Moody wrote about this:

> One of the excuses given in this parable was that the man He invited had bought a piece of ground and had to look

> at it. It was a lie, for he ought to have looked at it before he bought it. Then the next man said he'd bought some oxen and must prove them. That was another lie. If he hadn't proved them before he bought them, he should have and could have done it after the supper just as well as before it. But the third man had the silliest, the worst excuse of all. He said he had married a wife and couldn't come. Why didn't he bring her with him?[18]

One thing that Moody adds to this is about the lies we come up with when God asks us to do something. We *believe* lies, often, but we *tell* them as well, especially as it relates to making excuses.

In the Garden of Eden, just three chapters into the Bible, man and woman sinned. It's a good story and explains the Great Fall, but look at Adam and Eve's response, from Genesis 3:12–14, when God asks them to explain their behavior:

> The man said, 'The woman whom You gave to be with me, she gave me some of the fruit of the tree, and I ate.' Then the Lord God said to the woman, 'What is this that you have done?' And the woman said, 'The serpent deceived me, and I ate.'

Accuse God, accuse the wife, accuse the Deceiver, and somehow it exonerates the sinner. Psychologists might call it transference. Simply put, it's blaming someone else for our failures and our sins.

**PRAYER**

*Lord, forgive me for making excuses. I honestly stand now surrendering myself to You.*

18. D. L. Moody, *Sovereign Grace; or, The Redeemer's Invitation* (Grand Rapids, MI: Fleming R. Revell, 1891).

## DISCUSSION

1. What excuses have you made when you didn't want to do something you should do?
2. Have you ever made excuses for doing something wrong or against God's direction?

## MORE FOOD FOR THOUGHT

1. Read Romans 1:18–23. What excuse does mankind have for being estranged from God?

## DAY 31

*When the Advocate comes, whom I will send to you from the Father—the Spirit of truth who goes out from the Father—he will testify about me. And you also must testify, for you have been with me from the beginning. (John 15:26-27)*

Twice in elementary school, I got in trouble for defending someone else. Once I protected a girl who was being bullied on the playground. Another time, a friend was being belittled by a teacher. I got punished for throwing rocks at the bullies and I got in-school detention for speaking disrespectfully to the teacher. In both cases, though I am sorry for my methods, I do not regret my actions.

In this part of the speech, Jesus gives another name for the Holy Spirit. Previously He was called Comforter, Helper, and Spirit of Truth. Some believe that these names are synonymous, sharing the same function, but I believe here the name Advocate means something a little different.

The definition of "advocate" is one who pleads for another—one who speaks up for others who cannot speak for themselves. In politics and in law enforcement, an advocate may picket or argue for or against a cause. Does the Holy Spirit function this way?

Imagine the picture of a guilty person in court being represented by a lawyer. The accused and the lawyer stand before a judge, waiting for a verdict and a sentence. Superimpose that picture taking place in heaven. God is the judge, Jesus is the Advocate, we are the accused. Now imagine Jesus standing before God and declaring you guilty (because you are) and the Advocate says, "Your honor, this person is guilty, yes, but I will take the punishment and allow the defendant to go free."

That is not only advocacy, but it is substitution for penalty declared. Jesus, being the Son, is about to be crucified, resurrected, and then ascended back to heaven. So, the Holy Spirit will take His place in the court, reminding the Judge that the Son has already taken the punishment.

This probably confused the disciples at first, but later (at Pentecost) they would understand this. His flesh will be seen no more, but His Spirit will remain and "remind" God that He died for this guilty one.

Paul the apostle picks up this theme when he writes,

> And he who searches our hearts knows the mind of the Spirit, because the Spirit intercedes for God's people in accordance with the will of God. (Romans 8:27)

The gospel writer, John, also wrote in his open letter to the Jews scattered around the world.

> My dear children, I write this to you so that you will not sin. But if anybody does sin, we have an advocate with the Father—Jesus Christ, the Righteous One. He is the atoning sacrifice for our sins, and not only for ours but also for the sins of the whole world. (1 John 2:1)

**PRAYER:**

*God, Jesus, and Holy Spirit, I thank You for interceding for me to be declared "not guilty."*

**DISCUSSION:**

1. Do you believe that the Holy Spirit speaks to God on your behalf?

2. What does the Holy Spirit say about you?

**MORE FOOD FOR THOUGHT**

1. Read 1 John 2:1–2. What happens if we sin? Read 1 John 1:9. How can we be restored to fellowship with God after we sin?

## DAY 32

*These things I have spoken to you so that you will not be led into sin. They will ban you from the synagogue, yet an hour is coming for everyone who kills you to think that he is offering a service to God. These things they will do because they have not known the Father nor Me. But these things I have spoken to you, so that when their hour comes, you may remember that I told you of them. However, I did not say these things to you at the beginning, because I was with you. (John 16:1-4)*

The final chapter recorded of Jesus' table talk may seem redundant, and it is. The reason for that was that He wanted to make sure that His audience remembered some very important things. It was like these were bullet points for the whole speech.

"...so that you will not be led into sin..." was a warning and a reminder to stay the course no matter what happens. He knew He was leaving them, and that while He was with them, He could protect them from His enemies. But now, going away, He wanted them to beware of every pitfall. The road for them was going to be hard. They would be ostracized and excommunicated and suffer physically for their faith. Of course, the Holy Spirit would comfort them and encourage them and teach them, but despite that they had to remain steadfast in their ministries.

Even though in our lives we probably won't be beaten or killed for our faith, there are many in our world, in other countries, who will be. Our difficulty will be that we will be ridiculed and rejected by friends who refuse to believe in God. Though it may seem that *we* are being persecuted, *they* are really God-haters. We should not be surprised at this. It's part of the believer's walk. Jesus said so.

Paul, the apostle, started on the other side of persecution. He was the one persecuting the new believers. And yet, God used this man, after dramatically calling him, to do mighty things for the kingdom. Being ridiculed for our faith should not make us ashamed. Instead, it should strengthen our faith, because we know we are doing what God wants us to do.

Paul writes in Romans 1:16 "…I am not ashamed of the gospel, for it is the power of God for salvation to everyone who believes…."

An early 20th century Scottish pastor once prayed, "When we long for life without difficulties, remind us that oaks grow strong in contrary winds and diamonds are made under pressure."

### PRAYER

*Father, I will not be ashamed of my faith in You. I know that I may suffer for taking a stand, but I know that You will give me strength to endure.*

### DISCUSSION

1. What does it mean to be persecuted? Why will we be persecuted?
2. What should you do when someone makes fun of you for your commitment to God?

### MORE FOOD FOR THOUGHT

1. Read Matthew 5:1–11 (The Beatitudes). Notice what Jesus says about being persecuted. What is His promise?

## DAY 33

*But now I am going to Him who sent Me; and none of you asks Me, 'Where are You going?' But because I have said these things to you, grief has filled your heart. But I tell you the truth: it is to your advantage that I am leaving; for if I do not leave, the Helper will not come to you; but if I go, I will send Him to you. And He, when He comes, will convict the world regarding sin, and righteousness, and judgment: regarding sin, because they do not believe in Me; and regarding righteousness, because I am going to the Father and you no longer are going to see Me; and regarding judgment, because the ruler of this world has been judged. (John 16:5-11)*

Jesus senses that the disciples are (or will be) grieving. We all will experience grief at some point in our lives. It is inevitable because of the fragility of our bodies. Our loved ones will get sick, some will die. We, ourselves, will suffer from illness and impending death. So how can we survive it?

Counselors tell us that grief is a process. And they tell us that everyone grieves differently. The steps, they say, include (in no particular order) denial, anger, bargaining, depression, acceptance. Maybe it is some consolation that the loved one is with God in heaven, or that one day God will "...wipe away every tear from their eyes; and there will no longer be any death; there will no longer be any mourning, or crying, or pain...." (Revelation 21:4). It may be God's words through Jeremiah that bring comfort "...for I will turn their mourning into joy. And comfort them and give them joy for their sorrow" (Jeremiah 31:13). But this sentiment may not bring you comfort at all. In fact, it's likely that the disciples were in mourning for quite a while after Jesus went back to heaven, even after they were filled with the Holy Spirit. I'm sure they still missed their beloved Teacher. They maybe had to wait until they saw Him face to face. This idea may have prompted the lyrics to an older hymn:

*Sometimes the day seems long,*
*Our trials hard to bear.*

*We ŕe tempted to complain,*
*to murmur and despair.*
*But Christ will soon appear*
*to catch his bride away!*
*All tears forever over*
*in God's eternal day!*
*It will be worth it all when we see Jesus*
*Life's trials will seem so small when we see Christ;*
*One glimpse of His dear face all sorrow will erase*
*So bravely run the race till we see Christ.*

During grieving, try to remember Jeremiah's words in Lamentations 3:31–32:

> For the Lord will not reject forever, For if He causes grief, Then He will have compassion. In proportion to His abundant mercy.

And this from the psalmist:

> Though he brings grief, he will show compassion, so great is his unfailing love. (Psalm 23:4)

**PRAYER:**

*Lord, please walk with me during times of grief. Help me to feel Your presence as I travel this road.*

**DISCUSSION:**

1. Why do Christians suffer grief? Are we the only ones who have felt or will feel sorrow?

2. What can we do when grief comes?

## MORE FOOD FOR THOUGHT

1. Read Psalm 56:8. Does this give you comfort during times of grief?

## DAY 34

*I have many more things to say to you, but you cannot bear them at the present time. But when He, the Spirit of truth, comes, He will guide you into all the truth; for He will not speak on His own, but whatever He hears, He will speak; and He will disclose to you what is to come. He will glorify Me, for He will take from Mine and will disclose it to you. All things that the Father has are Mine; this is why I said that He takes from Mine and will disclose it to you. John 16:12-15*

Blind trust. It's a term we often use to explain the idea of following Jesus even when we don't understand His methods or His plans for us. When Jesus is promising the disciples that the "Spirit of Truth" is coming, He adds that the Spirit will guide them. He knew that He wouldn't be with them in the flesh, but that the Spirit will not only be with them but will be in them to keep them from losing their way.

That's His promise to us still, that the Spirit of Truth would teach us and would keep us on the right path. To know where the Spirit leads, we must listen to the right voice. And how do we do that?

Both of our sons have been on high school wrestling teams at some point. And being the loving, supportive parents that we are, we attended most of their matches. And it was agonizing.

As a spectator/supporter, a parent must sit semi-quietly and watch her son's body get twisted into positions she never thought possible. And the noise! Fans and competitors yelling at the tops of their lungs to "shoot the half" or whatever. And there were cheerleaders, too. Did you know that some schools have cheering squads for wrestling teams? Ours did. They not only scream and chant but also pound the gym floor in support. What chaos!

At one tournament with multiple schools participating, I tried to detach from the chaos as best I could so to preserve some energy and sanity. It was hard but for brief stints I was able to focus on one thing. One of these times I chose to watch our team's coach. I'd never really watched him before mostly because he was a gentle, unassuming man by nature, and he didn't often draw attention to himself. But what I saw him do that day made a lasting impression on me.

Coach was often down on his hands and knees almost at eye level with our boys —watching, evaluating, and admonishing, but not loudly at all. Just in a normal tone. I wondered: how could those guys hear their coach's voice above all the rest? And then it hit me.

This coach had worked with some of his team members for many years and so the guys recognized his voice. He had also led his team to many state championships, and it was obvious he knew the sport. The boys trusted him.

> I will lead the blind by ways they have not known, along unfamiliar paths I will guide them; I will turn the darkness into light before them and make the rough places smooth. These are the things I will do; I will not forsake them. (Isaiah 42:16)

## PRAYER

*Father, I will listen to Your voice and obey Your commands. I want to know and recognize Your voice clearly.*

## DISCUSSION

1. What "voices" do you hear that is calling you to do something?

2. How do you know that those voices are the Truth?

### MORE FOOD FOR THOUGHT

1. Read John 10:1–18. How can we recognize God's voice over others?

## DAY 35

*"A little while, and you no longer are going to see Me; and again a little while, and you will see Me." So some of His disciples said to one another, "What is this that He is telling us, 'A little while, and you are not going to see Me; and again a little while, and you will see Me'; and, 'because I am going to the Father'?" So they were saying, "What is this that He says, 'A little while'? We do not know what He is talking about." Jesus knew that they wanted to question Him, and He said to them, "Are you deliberating together about this, that I said, 'A little while, and you are not going to see Me, and again a little while, and you will see Me'?" (John 16:16-19)*

Could this be any more confusing? Even the discples didn't understand what Jesus was saying—which was not that unusual. The words that repeat are the focus here. "A little while." How long is that? When will it begin? How long will it last?

When trying to answer a child's question about the passing of time, sometimes we tell them in "three sleeps" an event will happen. It's because that's measurable to a child. That's tangible. But there are many things that we cannot measure in sleeps. And at this time in Jesus' timeline, He had to generalize this because there were so many variables that He could not reveal to them. He just wanted them, and us, to be ready for the next thing. The crucifixion, the resurrection, the ascension would come rather quickly in those men's current lives. The Second Coming, however, is for us to ponder. It hasn't come to pass yet. Many have tried to predict His return, but it's still pending. There's no way to know the exact date.

> The kingdom of God is not coming with signs that can be observed; nor will they say, 'Look, here it is!' or 'There it is!' (Luke 17:20)

Even Jesus Himself did not know the exact date. Matthew records this from His lips.

Matthew (in the 24th chapter of his Gospel) also addresses this question about His return:

> But about that day and hour no one knows, not even the angels of heaven, nor the Son, but the Father alone. (Matthew 24:36)
>
> Therefore, be on the alert, for you do not know which day your Lord is coming (v. 42)
>
> For this reason, you must be ready as well; for the Son of Man is coming at an hour when you do not think He will. (v. 44)

There may be one sleep…or two…or ten thousand. So, be ready.

### PRAYER

*Jesus, I want to be ready when You return. Help me to remember that You are coming back, and it is not possible for me to know when.*

### DISCUSSION

1. Does anyone know when Jesus will return to earth?

2. How can you be ready to see Him?

### MORE FOOD FOR THOUGHT

1. Read Matthew 24:1–31. What does Jesus say about His return?

## DAY 36

*Truly, truly I say to you that you will weep and mourn, but the world will rejoice; you will grieve, but your grief will be turned into joy! Whenever a woman is in labor, she has pain, because her hour has come; but when she gives birth to the child, she no longer remembers the anguish because of the joy that a child has been born into the world. Therefore, you too have grief now; but I will see you again, and your heart will rejoice, and no one is going to take your joy away from you. (John 16:20–22)*

Jesus uses the metaphor of the pains and joys of childbirth, although it might have seemed strange to hear Him talk about such things to this group of men. But this was a way to illustrate what was to come. There would be pain (grief and despair of His death) and then the delight of His resurrection and return. Two thousand plus years later, we have a different perspective on these words. The psalmist writes this long before Jesus walked the earth. "Weeping may last for the night, but a shout of joy comes in the morning." (Ps. 30:5)

Joy is a tiny word that is truly complex.

All my life as a believer, I've heard that there's a difference between happiness and joy. The distinction is that happiness is because of happenings, they say. But joy is something else. After doing a little digging I found several expressions for that tiny word.

Christian apologist Josh McDowell says, "My joy in life is not because I have not had any problems. I have joy because I have learned there is nothing too great for God's power to deal with, nor anything too small or insignificant for His love to be concerned about."[19]

From a website called The Bible Project that I trust, this is a good way to look at the idea of joy:

19. Josh McDowell, *Lecture and Teaching on Christian Joy.*

> Christian joy is a profound decision of faith and hope in the power of Jesus' own life and love. And that's what biblical joy is all about.[20]

And from R.C. Sproul:

> Sometimes we struggle to grasp the biblical view of joy because of the way it is defined and described in Western culture today. In particular, we often confuse joy with happiness.
>
> It is anxiety that robs us of our joy. And what is anxiety but fear? Fear is the enemy of joy. It is hard to be joyful when we are afraid.
>
> The true definition of joy goes beyond the limited explanation presented in a dictionary—'a feeling of great pleasure and happiness.' True joy is a limitless, life-defining, transformative reservoir waiting to be tapped into. It requires the utmost surrender and, like love, is a choice to be made.
>
> There are these two sides to experiencing joy, but both need to be considered when seeking joy: it is a gift and also a choice.[21]

## PRAYER

*God, in spite of my circumstances, I choose joy because I know that it comes from You.*

## DISCUSSION

1. Have you ever had a disappointment, and it made you unhappy?

---

20. The Bible Project. "Christian Joy Is a Profound Decision of Faith and Hope in the Power of Jesus' Own Life and Love." *BibleProject*. Accessed January 26, 2026. https://bibleproject.com/

21. From Compassion International (https://www.compassion.com/blog/famous-quotes-about-children/).

2. Have you ever known someone that you believed was joyful through a bad experience?

3. From where does that kind of joy come?

## MORE FOOD FOR THOUGHT

1. Read Romans 15:13 and Galatians 5:22–23. How does this illustrate the concept of joy?

## DAY 37

*And on that day, you will not question Me about anything. Truly, truly I say to you, if you ask the Father for anything in My name, He will give it to you. Until now you have asked for no thing in My name; ask and you will receive, so that your joy may be made full. (John 16:23-24)*

If this statement wasn't important, I think that Jesus wouldn't have repeated it. So, why is this concept so significant that He brings it up again?

What's in a name? Why does it matter if we ask in His name?

> The name of Christ is both the passport by which the disciples may claim access into the audience chamber of God and the medium through which the Divine answer comes.[22]

Have you ever been invited to a formal event? You probably were sent an invitation that was your admission. Maybe you didn't know everybody who would attend, but apparently you could gain access through the host—the one in whose name you present yourself.

One Bible commentator put it this way, "A name was a point of access, and naming and/or having knowledge of a name was thought to give one person power over another."[23]

So, look at it this way. It's God's "party," and Jesus is the "host." You can't get in without presenting yourself with the proper "credentials," and that is using the name of Jesus.

Alistair Begg tells a great fictional story about one of the two men hanging with Jesus on the cross. One cursed Jesus and mocked Him. The other asked for forgiveness and entrance into heaven. Begg imagines that the man whom Jesus forgave and would allow into paradise having a conversation at the entrance into heaven.

---

22. *NIV Application Commentary* © 2000 Gary M. Burge.
23. James George Frazer, *The Golden Bough*. Abridged ed., (New York, NY: Macmillan, 1922).

"Why should I let you into heaven?

"I don't know," the man replied.

The angel says, "You don't know? Uh…. Let me get my supervisor."

The angel gets his supervisor angel, who asks, "So, we've just a few questions for you. First of all, are you clear on the doctrine of justification by faith?"

The guy says, "I've never heard of it in my life."

"Have you ever been in a Bible study?

"No."

"Ever been baptized? Member of a church?"

"No."

"How did you make it here?"

The thief was stumped.

Finally, the angel asked, "On what basis are you here?"

And the man said, "The man on the middle cross said I can come."

You won't find this story in the Bible like this, but the concept is there. *The man on the middle cross said I could come.* He was personally invited to this great place, and his only reason for being there was that he came by Jesus' invitation. That was all he needed.

Asking the Father in Jesus' name is much the same. You use your relationship with Him to be able to come before God and ask Him anything. Anything at all.

In this passage, much like the one before it in this same speech, expecting God to give you whatever you want is not what this means. Like a good parent won't give his child something that is harmful or unseemly, God is the same with us. Accept His invitation, and enter into your reward using His name.

### PRAYER

*Jesus, I accept Your invitation to be with You always. I know that You have my best interest at heart. Therefore, I will follow You forever.*

### DISCUSSION

1. Have you ever been invited to a party or to an event and felt honored to be on the guest list?

2. What if you didn't accept the invitation, and you missed a wonderful opportunity?

3. How can you get to be invited to be in heaven?

### MORE FOOD FOR THOUGHT

1. Read Matthew 7:7–11. What do you learn about approaching the Father with a request?

## DAY 38

*These things I have spoken to you in figures of speech; an hour is coming when I will no longer speak to you in figures of speech, but will tell you plainly about the Father. On that day you will ask in My name, and I am not saying to you that I will request of the Father on your behalf; for the Father Himself loves you, because you have loved Me and have believed that I came forth from the Father. I came forth from the Father and have come into the world; again, I am leaving the world and going to the Father. (John 16:25-28)*

What is a figure of speech? There are many, but two of them often used by Jesus are metaphor and simile (comparing one thing to another) to make a point. Simile constructions use the words "like" or "as." Metaphor constructions do not. Jesus used these figures of speech to explain some very deep subjects for which His followers might struggle. The parables of Jesus are often used to explain God's love and acceptance. One such example that He uses, the parable of the Prodigal Son is found in Luke 15. In this chapter, Jesus compares God's love to the love of a father for a wayward child. It helped His audience, then and now, to have even a glimpse of what it's like to be accepted when we stray.

These figures of speech helped people understand, apply, and experience His message. In the Sermon on the Mount in Matthew 5–7, Jesus used examples of salt (5:13), light (5:14), lamps and baskets (5:15), moths and rust (6:20), birds (6:26), and flowers (6:28).

Why would He do this? Did He think that we're not smart enough to get the point? Maybe, but He did know that we might have a problem deciphering the language of heaven, and so He translated it into earthly terms so that there would be no mistake relating to His mission. "The Kingdom of Heaven is like"...a mustard seed (Matthew 13:31), yeast (Matthew 13:33), hidden treasure (Matthew 13:44).

I also think that Jesus used this method of teaching because He wanted us to seek, to search the meaning, to wonder about Him. Isn't that just like Him to lead us further into His word and His ways? Often, these kinds of searches leave us with more questions than answers. Exactly. I like that part. With many questions, we might **1)** realize that we don't know everything and that **2)** He won't explain everything in this life. Some truths we have to dig for. And often we won't have our answers revealed to us for a while—if ever—until we can ask Him when we see Him in heaven.

It's clear, however, that when He called these men, the disciples, to follow Him, they didn't ask Him where this would lead. Where they would be traveling. Where they would stay. What they would be eating. They just followed, and as they went, they probably had more questions than answers, and that's why they kept following Him. To learn more.

### PRAYER

*Father, please help me to keep exploring Your message, even when it seems a little cryptic. I want to keep seeking and learning more about You every day.*

### DISCUSSION

1. Would you follow someone even if you didn't know where you were going?

2. Is it wrong to have questions?

3. If you don't understand Jesus' figures of speech, what do you do?

### MORE FOOD FOR THOUGHT

1. Read John 21. The risen Jesus appears to His disciples. The subject of love came up in His conversation with Peter on the seashore. What did Jesus say about Peter's love for Him?

## DAY 39

*His disciples said, 'See, now You are speaking plainly and are not using any figure of speech. Now we know that You know all things, and* that *You have no need for anyone to question You; this is why we believe that You came forth from God.' Jesus replied to them, 'Do you now believe?' (John 16:29-31)*

We don't know which disciple made this statement. Maybe they all thought it, but only one, apparently, spoke it. Though they didn't all know the full impact of His mission, they were starting to get it—or so they thought. They said they believe that Jesus came from God. That belief would become one of the foundations of their faith, a foundation that they would build on through the coming years.

In college, I was required to take a lot of classes. Many of them didn't seem to be necessary to equip me for my chosen career, but I had to take them anyway. Even on the last day of class, the course wasn't over. There was the final exam. The grade on the test, added to my other grades, would determine whether I passed or not.

This is sort of what I get from this part of the speech. These men had learned a lot and had passed many of the daily quizzes, but they would have a big test in just a few hours that all of them would fail. They thought they were prepared, but the crucifixion of their Lord was not supposed to be on the test. They felt confident at first, even saying so by this statement "...You are speaking plainly,..." but Jesus wanted to let them know that even though they were getting closer to understanding His words, the course was far from over. The events to follow would turn their world (all the world, actually) upside down. There would be a new theological order, and, after Pentecost, the picture in their minds would become clearer relating to His words and His purpose. In academic terms this would be the difference between learning to read and comprehending what is read.

There's still so much to learn. We may struggle to comprehend, but the words may sound like gibberish. It's all right to not know everything. In fact, it should be exciting that we're having truth unveiled to us a little at a time. Our job is to receive those revelations as they come and remain thirsty to get more.

### PRAYER

*God, I don't understand a lot, but I know You have much to teach me. Open my eyes and my heart to see You at work.*

### DISCUSSION

1. Do you believe that Jesus was God's Son?

2. Do you believe that you have strayed away from God?

### MORE FOOD FOR THOUGHT

1. Read Mark 9. What had just happened when Jesus encountered the father of a demon-possessed son. Notice in verse 24 what the father asked Jesus. Can you relate to this statement?

## DAY 40

*Behold, an hour is coming, and has already come, for you to be scattered, each to his own home, and to leave Me alone; and yet I am not alone, because the Father is with Me. These things I have spoken to you so that in Me you may have peace. In the world you have tribulation but take courage; I have overcome the world. (John 16:32-33)*

The final words to His disciples. From this point on, He spoke only to His Father, in short responses to His accusers, and to those who saw Him resurrected and walking among them. The time of teaching them with words was over. Now it was time for His actions to support and reveal His true purpose.

He would be arrested, falsely accused, beaten, and sentenced to death by crucifixion. This execution was a Roman custom, and it was invented to be more than cruel. Doctors have studied to find that the human body can take just so much abuse before it shuts down. In Jesus' case, the blood loss related to the beatings was enough to kill Him, but hanging on a cross was even worse. Sometimes it would take days for a person to die. Jesus, however, died within a few hours. Before the sun went down and the Sabbath began, He spoke seven last sentences to the Father. The next to last was, "It is finished." His work of giving Himself as a sacrifice was done. Now the resurrection, His appearance to many, and His ascension would complete the circle.

And so, we're here, centuries later, trying to make sense of this time in history. So much of it has to do with reading eyewitness accounts of this process. It was prophesied in the Old Testament and written about throughout the scriptures. The questions we have about it may never be answered, but like so much of the path to salvation, we must believe and accept by faith.

Go back and read this after-dinner speech and try to take it out of its historical context and read as if you are learning about it for the first time and He is speaking only to you. Imagine that He is appearing to you after His resurrection.

Paul, who was a later apostle, wrote this to people in Rome...

> If you confess with your mouth Jesus *as* Lord, and believe in your heart that God raised Him from the dead, you will be saved; for with the heart *a person* believes, resulting in righteousness, and with the mouth he confesses, resulting in salvation." (Romans 10:9–10)

### PRAYER

*Father, there's so much that I don't understand about You and about Your Son, Jesus. However, I accept by faith that You have given me a way to live for You and to be with You even after I die.*

### DISCUSSION

1. Do you believe that Jesus was sent to bring you back?

2. Do you want to be with God forever? How can you do that?

### MORE FOOD FOR THOUGHT

1. Read Mark 4:35–41, the account of Jesus calming the sea during a sudden storm. Compare this with Psalm 46. What do these chapters teach you about the storms of life?

## TAKE OUT

A few times, when I was a child and didn't finish a meal I had ordered at a restaurant, my mother would say, "your eyes were bigger than my stomach." I took that to mean that when I had ordered from a menu, I had underestimated my digestive capacity. Sometimes I'd take the leftovers in a "doggy bag" or to-go box. Well, at the Lord's Supper table, there was probably little or no food leftovers, but there were many things spoken at the meal that would linger in the minds of those who heard Jesus' words. Hopefully they would ruminate on them and digest them later. After reading and studying these devotionals you may still be hungry for more of Jesus' words of wisdom. These would be nourishment for the soul.

Craving God's Word is something I'd like to experience. I do read it and digest it, but I don't always feel that I can't survive without it, mostly because I've never been in a situation where I was deprived of access to it. There were Bibles everywhere in our home and I was at the church house every time the doors were open. Maybe that's why I haven't longed for it more. I pray that you and I will become hungrier and thirstier for Him than ever before.

Join me at the table and feast on the delicious smorgasbord to which God has invited us.

In a little while I'll have another book published based on a similar premise. *Fresh from the Mountain* will contain forty days of devotionals based on Jesus' Sermon on the Mount.

## Bibliography

### Bible

The Holy Bible, New American Standard Bible (2020). La Habra, CA: The Lockman Foundation. *(Scripture quotations are taken from the NASB unless otherwise noted.)*

### Books

Begg, Alistair. *The Christian Manifesto*. Chicago: Moody Publishers.

Elliot, Elisabeth. *Through Gates of Splendor*. Wheaton, IL: Tyndale House.

Evans, Tony. *Prayer and the Kingdom*. Chicago: Moody Publishers.

Keller, Timothy. *Prayer: Experiencing Awe and Intimacy with God*. New York: Dutton.

Lewis, C. S. *Mere Christianity*. New York: HarperOne.

MacArthur, John. *The MacArthur New Testament Commentary: John 12–21*. Chicago: Moody Publishers.

McDowell, Josh. *More Than a Carpenter*. Wheaton, IL: Tyndale House.

Swindoll, Charles R. *Living Above the Level of Mediocrity*. Dallas: Word Publishing.

Wiersbe, Warren W. *Be Transformed (Romans)*. Colorado Springs: David C. Cook.

### Articles & Media

The Bible Project. "Joy." *BibleProject*. Accessed January 2026. https://bibleproject.com.

*Christianity Today*. Accessed January 2026. https://www.christianitytoday.com.

### Hymns

Spafford, Horatio G. "It Is Well with My Soul." 1873.

Made in the USA
Monee, IL
13 April 2026

47841617R00073